Blue Shades Publishing Inc.

380 Redwood Lane NW, Unit C

Concord, North Carolina 28027

www.blueshadespublishing.com

ISBN: 979-8-9887958-7-2

FROM JOY TO MOURNING

A mother's journey on the battlefield
fighting the wars right here at home.

FROM JOY TO MOURNING

A mother's journey on the battlefield
fighting the wars right here at home.

For every tear that's fallen from the eyes of those who've lost a loved one due to gun violence, this book is dedicated to you. For every ounce of unspoken pain endured in the twilight. For every second, minute and hour of the day you've felt trapped inside the palms of grief. Know that we see ourselves in you. That we align ourselves to fight with you and for you. That we pray for you and ask that you pray justice is served for the life of De'Mar Bester. Keep God first. Keep loved ones close. Live everyday like it's your first and the last. De'Mar continues to be a lighthouse shimmering bright as we journey forward. Your watermark of love can be seen on your daughter's faces and felt through the stories speaking to your selfless generosity. You are forever loved. We will fulfill the promises we made to you. We love you. Amen.

Written by Darwin Gray

story to tell. I didn't start out on this journey to say, "here's my journey." Like others, circumstances led me on my journey.

Othea Stevenson

Isaiah 43: ¹⁸ "Forget the former things;
do not dwell on the past.
¹⁹ See, I am doing a new thing!
Now it springs up; do you not perceive it?
I am making a way in the wilderness.

I met this man on Black People Meet.com. I had over 700 messages before I initially seen this man. After about two months, I again viewed his profile. There was something different about him. He actually looked very happy dressed in a white 2-piece suit and standing on a cruise ship. I began to look at his profile more closely. This was around the 17th of July of 2013. I told myself that I was tired of these men not being the man that God created. I questioned, should I keep looking or should I just give up on love, finding my King. I took a chance and decided to look just to see what lame stuff he might have in his profile. The title of his profile read "Cautious", that made me very curious, what does he mean "Cautious"? Was it a woman that hurt him or was he leary about all the lies on this site? Inquiring minds (mine anyway) wanted to know.

So, as I begin to read his profile, it said "a man not ashamed to say he loves the Lord, and he has a testimony." It's getting deep, I told myself. Everything I wanted to hear was in his profile. I need to get up enough nerve to message him to see if he would respond. Wow! He responded, in a very respectable way. I was amazed, this is really okay, so I messaged him again, and we went back and forth for about a week. I felt that this might not be a bad thing, after all we held each other's attention. My next step was to get up enough guts to give my phone number. I did and he called, but I missed his call and listened to the voice mail he left, OMG! A soothing voice (Thank You Lord), now what, I wanted to be relaxed when I talk to this one.

before I dialed his number. I finally got up enough courage to do so, thank you Lord, he answered, and once again that soothing voice which calmed my spirit for some reason began to work its magic. Unfortunately, he was on his way to the movies and asked could he call me back. I said hmm phone tag, but I respected that he asked if it would be okay, so I said that's fine. True to his word he did call me back. He was picking up something to eat which of course in my mind proved the fact he was single. He shared with me that he plays softball, enjoys going to the movies, and is active in church.

I asked him to take a picture of himself and he did which was funny because he stops some people he didn't even know and asked them to take it. I like that, spontaneous and take control. Then we really started having a good conversation. I was surprised at myself, but I liked it. As we got more into asking questions about each other I noticed we had a lot in common. I said really, a man who actually likes what I liked and sounds humble and true. I went into asking him about his profile and he told me he was going through a divorce, but it wasn't final yet. Now this scares me because I like him a lot and he sound kind and considerate. Do I hang on or cut my losses? If you know me, I start praying asking God why? What's this about? Listening to see what God tells me. The conversation continues, and he even offers to drive to see me. Really, wow that's nice he doesn't mind the distance he has to travel.

Now this man is going to travel (2 hours) to see me, imagine that and so soon, we've only talked for a few weeks on the phone. He wants to come on a weekday which is fine he's retired so I guess he got all the time in the world (lol). I agree to let him, which I'm skeptical he'll even come. Men say a lot, but do they always follow through, no they don't. Tuesday comes around, and he calls to touch bases, he tells me that he's coming. In fact, he's actually on his way. I ask myself, "Do I really want this, and so soon?" The last date I was on was bad. Really bad. But there was some reason, it made me feel safe. Okay he's here! Is he going to act different, look different? I don't know, I'm just so nervous. Wow button down shirt nice jeans nice shoes impressive, professional looking.

Now, we do the cordial greeting, and he reaches over in my car and gives me a hug, that soothes the nerves. Time to go, (we met at McDonalds parking lot). He follows me to my house I give him a tour. You know I'm simple, he likes the house. So, we proceed by riding in my car out to eat. I pick Chinese because I remember him liking that but when we get to the restaurant he asks if I mind if we too went to Red Lobster instead. Wow, a man who speaks up and takes control, this is getting good ooh and I like that. He opens doors, such a gentleman even suggests something he likes from the menu, so I try what he likes it's all good, and the conversation is good as well. Before we get ready to leave, he suggests getting some wine, nice and smooth it will relax us and set a mood I don't know what mood, but I'll find out. We talk, we have so much in common I relax laying my head back on the couch and he leans over and kisses me. I'm shocked but really feeling this man soft lips but I'm screaming inside Lord I have not felt this feeling in a while help!!!!!!!!!!!!!!!!! Man, and he smells so good everything I liked, is this a joke am I being punked, or have I found my king?

Ephesians 3: [17] so that Christ may dwell in your hearts through faith. And I pray that you, being rooted and established in love, [18] may have power, together with all the Lord's holy people, to grasp how wide and long and high and deep is the love of Christ, [19] and to know this love that surpasses knowledge—that you may be filled to the measure of all the fullness of God.

As he kisses me, his lips, soft tongue, hands gently caressing my face. What a surprise. I get to rubbing his chest thinking man am I going too far? I started drinking more wine to take my mind off what might happen. We finished the wine then he kissed me again, and then I asked him "you want to go upstairs maybe listen to some music have a nice conversation. So, we go up to get ready for bed, I change downstairs he changes up we lay down and kiss some more I stroke his body, he strokes mine. I want it I'm overdue I trust him so I'm willing. He looks over and says he doesn't have condoms, so he offers to go get some, how sweet and responsible, so he gets up and leaves. Man, I'm wondering why am I doing this?

Pacing back and forth thinking okay this man has left to get condoms wow. I'm nervous saying to myself why am I allowing this to happen? Do I need it or is it a want? Minutes are going by, should I have let him go out there? He knows nothing about Decatur, but the store is only a few blocks from here, so I called him to ask if he was, okay? He said Walgreens was closed so he found a gas station and was on his way back. Wow he took another chance, it must be meant to be. Okay he's back I'm waiting by the door he smiles as if to say you ready for this. We went back upstairs and began kissing again.

I just melted in this man's arms. I was seriously feeling wanted, held, loved, I had so many emotions going on. This man was making love too me, holding me just the way I wanted to be held. How am I supposed to feel after what we just did, the first me? I felt so good so safe around this man but why? Lord have mercy on me. When he leaves will I be able to face him again? My heart was beating fast with all these thoughts but when I looked at him, he was at peace and comfortable. I kept wondering, did he really look at my body, did he like it, was he attractive to it? I didn't even think about him, I was attracted to his heart.

We rested peacefully, he actually held me in his arms and made me feel comfortable. Wow we put each other to sleep. It's something different about this man why do I feel safe and so good in his arms like I've been knowing him all my life? Man, I knew I had to get up early, but I didn't want to leave him, crazy right! I had been through so much I didn't want another man looking at me let lone touching me, I almost gave up till I met Jesse. Wow he looked so peaceful like he belonged next to me. I prayed for love and a king, is this him? I keep asking God is this you're doing. Are you allowing me to trust again or is this man like my past. I'm going to pray while he's sleeping. Then I'm going to sleep but not until I look at his body one more time, damn that looks good.

Well, the fun is over I decided yea, I better go to work. They count on me to be there no one in their right mind wants to deal with my classroom. Jesse said he would stay here until my break and that's cool, I trust him, what could he possibly take out of here without someone looking? People are always in your business even if it doesn't look like it. Off to work I go.

I Corinthians 13: ⁴ Love is patient, love is kind. It does not envy, it does not boast, it is not proud. ⁵ It does not dishonor others, it is not self-seeking, it is not easily angered, it keeps no record of wrongs. ⁶ Love does not delight in evil but rejoices with the truth. ⁷ It always protects, always trusts, always hopes, always perseveres. ⁸ Love never fails. But where there are prophecies, they will cease; where there are tongues, they will be stilled; where there is knowledge, it will pass away.

Well, I'm pulling in my driveway he's still here imagine that! Wow and he's up walking around good morning, Jesse he smiles and says good morning Othea how's work going? I said its work then he asked if I wanted to eat lunch before I went back to work, what a gentleman I thought so considerate. Sure, I'd loved to go to lunch, so we went to subways ordered and sat there to eat. He smiled at me as if he knew I was nervous and I was, I just didn't know what to think about this man, sweet tone of voice, smelling good, sexy character. Are we going to see each other after this?

Well, I must guide Jesse back to the highway. His GPS took him on some back roads to get here but he made it, and we had a good time. Now I'm waving him on, and I pray he makes it home safely. One thing about me is that I pray all the time. I always got God on my side, I told him to text me soon as he gets home, let's see if he follows directions. A lot of men are forgetful and do it later when it comes to mind not unless they're thinking about you, we will see which one he's on!

Two hours later he texts me saying he made it home safely, imagine that he must have been thinking about me or was that a need for him or a void he had to fill? I'll know because the longer we talk it will reveal itself. He also commented that he had a good time and thanked me for trusting him in my home, how sweet. He said he had a lot of work to do I really didn't get into asking him all that so far all I know is that he retired from the U.S. Coast

I'm watching this one its more to him that meets the eye.

John 6:35: [35] Then Jesus declared, "I am the bread of life. Whoever comes to me will never go hungry, and whoever believes in me will never be thirsty.

Well, Mr. Stevenson, my day went well, 25 students spitting and kicking, the norm for me. How was your day? He proceeded telling me that he also teaches at two different colleges, so in my mind I'm saying okay wow retired from the Coast Guard, and went back to work as an instructor nice, I like that. We then get on family. He tells me he has two children by his first wife, who is now deceased wow but were still young is my thought and I wanted to ask how she died but I would be prying in his business. I guess in due time it will come up again. He told me his children lived in Texas, and North Carolina and were grown.

Then of course we got on how many children I had I said three boys and one girl. He said I thought you had only two children. I said look on that site I'm sure everyone has some errors for real everything written isn't true and besides my daughter in law set that profile up for me. She wanted me to start dating again, I guess I deserved it after the abuse and stress I went through, but little did she know I can't even trust another man right away he'd have to do some serious proving.

I told him my children were also grown and gone, heck they were gone fresh out of high school before I could put them out, they were ready to move out. Tired of mom's rules I guess or I'm just too strict. It's something different about this man though. I've spoken with several which was a quick turn off for me I guess I'm picky, nope just older, and wiser. He also tells me he loves to play softball and his ex-wife as well "mmmmmmmmm" I really want to hear about this ex, why did she leave this man with such good qualities and a nice personality. Once again, I'm not going to pry but it will come up. We ended up talking for a couple of hours.

He had a lot of them. But something through the conversation I noticed he's a humble man and very spiritual at least that's what I'm hearing. We get into talking about our goals and some of the things I want to do in life. I have this bucket list I keep, one is a cruise, two is to fly, three is going to South Carolina (Myrtle Beach) and four is Wisconsin dells. I've been wanting to go there since I was a child, and the fifth one is a secret when it happens then I've accomplished it. Well, it's time to go to bed, me and him have been laughing and talking nonstop, wait a minute I'm actually laughing again and holding a good conversation with a man, I'm starting to like this.

Wow, going to bed at 11:30 pm last night sure is catching up with me this morning, but at least at my job I get a nice long break I can go home and take a nap and be refreshed all over again. I'm loving it. Man for some odd reason I got this man on my mind. Was the conversation good or do I need to see him again? He was pretty good or was I just in a vulnerable state? I should ask when the next time we're going to see each other but I'd be pushing it. I'll wait till he asks or invites me. I do have a few days coming up, my boys decided to cancel a trip to Minnesota after I took the time off. That would be nice then I can see how this man lives! So far so good everything he says I like, can't wait till he calls, or should I call him while I'm on break? Yea why not just to say good morning, what's the worst thing could happen, he just doesn't answer. Well, I tried calling him, he must be sleeping, so I'll leave a message. He's on my mind so much, that as soon as I lay down, I start thinking about that night and there goes my mind, drifting off.

Well still no answer and besides I need to get up and take a shower. I'm still in shock meeting a man online and it really feels good were communicating well, "hey'" hey" guess who's calling? You guessed it. Hi Jesse, how are you? You know that's an ice breaker to find out what he's been doing all day. He tells me he's been in his office working on grading papers for his students I'm thinking this man sounds awful busy so when does he find the time then he says if this friendship goes any further, I'll make time for you, that's what I'm talking bought! I asked him what's he doing in a few weeks. I have some time off. He replies saying nothing but schoolwork and I'm welcome to visit him anytime. "Wow" just what I wanted to hear. I want to see how this man lives; this will help my curiosity. If he's not clean then I better run now, I had a husband who got so used to me doing everything it became natural that he didn't want to do anything but work, lay on his back eat shit and drink on occasions. I don't want that again; I learned my lessons all too well. I plan to drive down to Shiloh and spend 3 days with Jesse, this will be interesting can't wait.

Proverbs 3: [23] Then you will go on your way in safety, and your foot will not stumble.

Well, the time has come, I'm all packed and ready to go. How far is Shiloh well I know Jesse said it's not far from St. Louis once I get close, I'm sure he'll guide me straight to his house. I noticed one thing about him he's very helpful and thoughtful. This drive will be a piece of cake, turn my music up and ride. I wonder what this man got planned for me. I should be worried, but I feel like I can trust him. Imagine that me trusting a man again. He is so humble. He probably lives in this 3-bedroom home with a white picket fence and a whole bunch of rose bushes around it. We'll be patient, he's very nice also. Okay it's been an hour and thirty minutes I better call him I'm getting close! Hey, Jesse, I'm thirty minutes away. What exit do I take? Exit 40 which will lead right towards Shiloh.

He told me when I got close to the address to call him because he wasn't at home. I'm going to surprise him and use my GPS to drive right up to the front door! You know me, I like surprises and I'm definitely an inquisitive person. Okay I'm at the address but I think my GPS got messed up and I'm at the wrong house, or am I? Okay I'm going to circle around and see what the GPS does. Wow it keeps leading me back to the same house. It's time to call Jesse. Hey Jesse, I think I'm at the wrong house, it looks like a white private neighborhood. He asked me what does the address says on the mailbox? I tell him it says 1213. Then he describes the front of the house OMG! It's his house. Did this man lead me on or what? I told him I didn't want a man who bragged about what he got! Wait a minute he didn't! I never asked because I liked the mere fact, he was spiritual, kind, and humble. What have I gotten myself into? I don't want a rich sketchy life; I've been there and done that. That's not for me anymore. Am I up, but I've got questions.

Here he comes, he's smiling I don't know why. Is it because I made it or he's saying surprise! I will just be patient and see what he says. I want to get in my car and drive off but it's too damn late and I don't drive at night. He gets out, opens the garage door and tells me to drive in. It's a lot of storage in the garage so I want to be careful. I drive in get out, he hugs me and says I'm so glad you made it. He asked where's my bags, so he could carry them in. I let him, then he took my hand and led me into his home. We reach the kitchen, it's beautiful but this is not what I signed up for.

You see, I have been through the ill-gotten gains before, and I know what it looks like, and I was afraid that this is what this was. Let's see how this goes. He gives me a tour, but my mind is on some negative stuff. I just don't want my life spiraling out of control at the hands of another man. I do not want anything to do with something gotten by illegal means. This man seemed too humble to have a home like this, or at least that was my impression of him. I promised God nothing else before him, and I'm going to make sure of that.

Well, the house is surely not a house I would expect from the man I met, this seems like it belongs to a totally a different person or is this an act? I'll find out soon enough. He puts my bags in his room, but he has 4 bedrooms. He suggested I could sleep in any room, imagine that. I said that at my house but all I have is 2 bedrooms. He takes my hand and says he has a surprise. He leads me back downstairs out to the garage and points to this car which is a Jaguar he just purchased. He wanted us to ride in style I guess (lol).

Okay, I'm really not feeling this, what is this man into? I was impressed with the humble man I met, was I lead on or what! Should I just sit back and relax but I'm hungry, so my next question is what's for dinner? His response is Texas roadhouse for an appetite. We went to dinner. It was nice, Jesse introduced me to the porkchop dinner. It was delicious and great company, can't ask for too much more right now! Well back to the house we go. I'm really trying to feel comfortable. Have you ever felt like something just isn't right, like you feel something coming on, but you don't know what! I'm so overwhelmed right now I need a prayer on top of a drink (lol). My last two dates were crazy. Now what's in store with this one and why didn't he tell me on the phone all what he had?

So, I asked Jesse why didn't you talk about your house and the new car you purchased? He answered, he wanted someone to be attracted to him for who he was not for what he had or how financially stable he is. Good answer but we talked for a while, and I rode up on this! Holding something like this back makes me feel leery what else are you hiding? It's dark now so there's no way I'm going to drive home tonight. He doesn't know yet that I don't drive on the highway at night but if this blossoms any further, he'll learn a lot about me.

He put on some music pulls a bottle of wine out of the refrigerator and asked would I like to sit on the patio and enjoy the breeze. Sure, nice gesture I hope he doesn't think he's going to get me drunk and take control of this sexy body. The music is right, I will say one thing, we really talk and laugh a lot which is good. If a man can't make you laugh and be serious when you need him to it's a waste of time. And if he can't cry in front of you and is prideful, I don't want you because he's going to put on an act and forget where his blessings come from.

I know that all too well. Man, I'm feeling good, nice breeze music jamming good conversation, no he's ain't, singing really! Wait a minute, he can sing. For real now he's over here dancing behind me. Either that wines getting to him or this man hasn't had none since the last time I seen him. But who's to say, we live a distance away and he living in this big house by himself. He might have a jump off coming when he needs it. That will come to the transpired but he feels good. Well wine all gone it's time to go in and get relaxed. At first, I was uncomfortable, but that wine relaxed my nerves. He asked did I want to get in something more comfortable, which was a good idea. I felt sticky driving in those clothes. I was so used to taking a shower every night at the same time, I was ready.

So, I took a shower. It felt good along with that wine I had running through my blood stream, so I lotion up put on my gown and jumped into this big bed. I noticed out of the corner of my eye on his nightstand was a machine that looked like a breathing machine of some sort. One thing about me I definitely pay attention to health and if a man isn't conscious of his health, nope I don't want him! If he doesn't care that means he might not be around long in my book. Yeah, I know God has that final say but let's take care of ourselves in the meantime. He noticed me looking and tells me he used to snore really bad and had sleep apnea. Wow the last guy I dated either was lazy or fell asleep at the drop of a dime. Please explain more Jesse. I sure wanted to know if this affected his health. But he assured me he was fine now, it was taken care of, that was nice to hear.

Then understanding that he is a retired veteran I'm sure he has good health benefits and hoping he stays on top of those doctors' appointments. He takes a shower next, so I lay there contemplating the mood we were getting ready to get in. One thing I enjoyed was talking to him. Here he comes smelling fresh and wiped down with cologne. One thing I don't like is when a man doesn't put up the effort to look good or smell good. We start talking a little about my past which draws out a very touchy subject about the abuse I've been through. As I tell him about my abusive past Jesse rises out of the bed and comes over and sits on my side of the bed, looks at me and says he wants to be honest with me. Okay when I hear those words blood starts to rush through my vein's, heart beating fast, and my first inner thought is, has this man been abused, has he abused women or what? Now wanted to choke me!

I sit still and wait for what's coming next. He proceeds by telling me when him and his wife separated, she put an order of protection on him and did it on his birthday. Now he said he has never put a hand on her. His mother taught him to respect woman, when it was time to go to court, she drops the order. So right now, you can imagine the look on my face. Should I get up and leave now or trust this man. Why did he tell me this? Is this going to come up or what? Too much for one day, what's next? Am I going to be able to sleep? Do I start praying now? All kinds of crazy thoughts are going through my head. He keeps pleading with me, saying he never laid a hand on her, the look in his eyes is more like a hurt look like he was scared to tell me. Now he's looking at me to respond, what do I say?

So, I tell him to go back and lay down, let's just rest. He knew he stirred up all kinds of thoughts, but he said he had to be honest. We lay there very silent, not getting any sleep, so after 15 minutes or so I asked him to tell me a story to take our minds off that! So, he tells me about when he first joined the Coast Guard and how young he was, then the only black man on a boat and all he could think of was the movie by Alex Haley *(who was also in the Coast Guard)* Roots. Back then it was common for whites to look at blacks like, why are you here? He was scared shitless, but they treated him fair, and he felt more comfortable as time went on. I know one thing, that trust thing either won't transpire, and I won't come back or start having a little faith to see where this goes. We talk a little more, laugh a lot, and the next thing you know he steals a kiss then says he's praying this relationship will work because he really likes me.

I told him it takes time let's just see what happens then he kisses me again but holds on much longer and takes his hands and rubs my lower back as if he's comforting me. He then pulls me close chest to breast then begins kissing down my neck with his hands moving all over my body. Now he feels good, and I feel like foreplay which literally turns me on. We make love and that's what we both needed, we take deep breathes after 35 minutes lay back, pull the cover up, hold each other and fall straight to sleep, damn that was good. The sun shines right through the windows, how do I know? He has no curtains up, just blinds. I look over and he's staring right at me, kind of scares me, but he said he's been watching me sleep. Ok I don't know whether to think that's weird or romantic.

Then he says you're beautiful when you rest it seems like you have a sense of peace. I said I do. I mean who doesn't when they sleep, he said a lot of people go to bed angry, not me I said. I'm done with those restless nights. He asked me what I would like for breakfast because he's cooking, how sweet. I told him to surprise me. Well, I found out one thing he's good at making breakfast. Anytime a man gets up and fixes breakfast it must have been good the night before (lol). We ate breakfast and sat there laughing and talking for a while. All of the sudden, the doorbell rings. I asked are you expecting someone he says no then he peeks out the window, you know how men do it when they got a so-called friend with benefits who won't let go. Low and behold it's his ex-wife! Yep ex-wife! Then he had the nerve to ask me if I wanted to meet her? Really!!!!!!!!!!!!!!!!!!!!!!!

Hell no, at least that's what I say in my mind, I'm not stupid you trying to get a divorce. Why do I need to meet her now and stir up some negative shit like he's always been involved with me. Nope I won't do it! She rings the bell a few more times then finally leaves. Personally, I think he wanted to make her jealous, he must remember she left him so already she been doing her own thing. She wouldn't have been jealous just got even $$$$$$ signs probably would have lit up in her eyes. Well, I'm sure she'll call in a minute to ask where he is. He is looking crazy, very awkward moment right! One thing I will say I'm glad he didn't open the door; some women can't take seeing another woman in her house, they snap and cause confusion. I know. I come from a family of 11

I'm going to go back upstairs and give him some time to think. Men always need time to gather thoughts.

The damage is already done. I'm just waiting to see what's the catch why did she leave? It's always two sides to a story. This kind and compassionate man, and you just up and leave don't come back for the rest of your things, and it's been over 2 years? Either he was abusive, and you're scared and that was your get away or you're cheating, and the other man or woman promised you the world and the sex is the bomb! The wife always makes it out to be the husband's fault. Point taken, she fell out of love with her husband. What's the old saying? She feels the grass is greener on the other side. All I can say is keep it moving just don't jump in my face, I'm not the one to be disrespected. I know one thing I've seen a man scorned before, they're worse than women! I'm just going to take my time and have fun. I've been through enough pain, and I'm not going through no more, too old for bullshit. Besides I'm divorced and God knows that was some serious pain.

The next day I met one of his brothers, Willie. Willie is next to the eldest in the family, there is one brother older than him. Jesse has three brothers, and three sisters. He is next to the youngest in the family. Jesse, his brother Willie, and I are in the car, and we are headed to Scott AFB *(military base where he shops for food, clothing and gets his medicine etc. as a retired military man)*. My dad always told me to marry a military man. He said the character and discipline they learn in the military will go a long way, and he is more likely to treat you right. Now it never dawned on me to ask Jesse what his rank in the military was, and since he is so humble and does not boast or brag, he never volunteered that information. As we drive onto the base, we must go through this gate, where there are armed guards who must check your ID to allow you on the base. So, we are just chit chatting, and as Jesse pulls up to the gate, he hands the man his ID. The man looks at his ID, gives it back to him, steps back and salutes Jesse. Ok, I'm impressed. I go what was that. His brother Willie is sitting in the tell you he was a Lieutenant Commander in the Coast Guard? I said no, he never mentioned it. Then Willie said, yeah Mama used to love seeing that. That's when Jesse said, yeah, she was proud to see that, and would tell everyone *"Did you know that they have to salute Jesse every time he comes on a military base"?* Jesse tears up when he discusses that about his mother. I can just see her beaming with pride as she watches them salute her son. I wish I would have had the chance to meet her.

Let me take you back a little to my past. I was married at a young age with two kids, graduated from high school dating my high school sweetheart whom I married. Two kids, both of us going to college him for engineering and me to be a teacher, something I've been wanting to be since I was five years old. I wanted to be three things when I grew up, a housewife and mother like June Cleaver and a teacher, guess what? I got to be all three, exciting right to be everything you wanted to be at a young age living the life fine husband tall, caramel skin tone, athletic build from running track and playing basketball and shy in his own special way. Which made him even more attractive to other women.

But I was one of them strong black girls with an athletic look, big brown oval shaped eyes, a birth mark on the left side of my face shaped like a strawberry, caramel skin complexion coke bottle shape and short hair but, kept a sexy style and a look of please don't disrespect me. I can be nice and sweet. But overall, we were good until our life took a complete turn that will make your head spin. My youngest brother went away to college to play football till he damaged his knee, preventing him from playing ball anymore, so he had to come home. Football is all he ever knew. He had two children that my mother was taking care of and that's a whole other story of how she's raising his children.

So, you can only imagine, he came home broke looking for a job and two kids to feed with just a high school diploma and some college credits. He wasn't getting nowhere, so he'd sit our porch for hours after applying for at least four jobs a day. Late one evening he and my then husband were sitting on the porch just chilling when they started to notice that some of the same people this housing complex copping drugs.

My brother said I wonder how much these drug dealers make in a night. He started asking around and someone suggested that he try it. My brother took his last $50 dollars and bought $50 worth of drugs, separated it into three bags and sold each for $20 dollars. He made a profit of $10 dollars in a matter of 20 minutes from just those three customers. Then he went back to a dealer and spent that $60 and made a profit of $40 dollars and it went on from there.

He eventually got his own package product. He had my husband experiment and my husband eventually learned to be one of the best chemists around, and that's where the trouble began. We had too much money and eventually too many customers, and addiction, when I say addiction, I mean using your own supply not snorting but crack cocaine smashing it and lacing it with weed. That is a serious addiction! Don't tell me marijuana and cocaine mixed isn't addictive because I lost a lot, including the ones I love, and I even got locked up.

Have you ever been so in love and so stupid that you will take the rap for your husband or your baby daddy thinking he'll do the right thing, stay out there take care of the kids stop selling dope and work to raise our family? Yep, I did that stupid shit. Federal time for not snitching. That could have caused me eight years, but they had no real evidence except for an ounce tapped underneath one of our cars and guess who was driving. I knew better to say it wasn't mines and they knew that. They had been watching us for two years and my husband definitely was a wimp in doing any prison time, so I depended on him to take care of our kids. But it never worked out like that! He kept selling, cheating, and family falling by the wayside. I took a plea of four years state time but before serving my time I got to come home from the county jail for two weeks because I had a family and had to make arrangements before I left.

the kids while I was in the county while he did his dirt. There's no way I could leave like this, and my kids not being taken care of. My husband and I started arguing about living a better life, but that addiction and the dope game got him so messed up that arguing gave him an excuse to leave every time. I had no one I could trust with my kids. I just sat on the floor and cried. I had truly hit rock bottom with one week left to place my kids in a safe place. Me and the kids took off and walked down by the corner store, where three women walked up on us.

I got one baby on my hip and three others on my side. Yep, four kids, three boys and one girl. The women stopped me as they were handing out some flyers about visiting their church, Antioch Missionary Baptist Church. That day the women said it would be a special program and there would be food afterwards. My mind kept saying, what will it hurt? I had lost so much already, I tried to give those women every excuse not to go but my mind wouldn't let me, it kept eating at me to go. So, I ended up going to church that Sunday. God must have known what he was doing, because He sat me next to a woman who was so kind and caring towards my kids. Toward the end of service, I walked up asking for prayer, for someone I could trust to help take care of my children as I had no family I could trust. I was unaware that the woman I sat next too would be the angel that God had sent my way.

It wasn't until Pastor Cheney, who has since passed on, asked me what I needed prayer for, and as I told him, he smiled and shared with me that the lady I was sitting next to was a foster parent. Her name was Ms. Elaine Houston. She walked up, held my hand and said she would do all she could do to help me with my children. I served my time with Ms. Houston by my side, helping me and taking care of my children while I was away.

It turns out that the federal government were not only watching me and my then husband, but they were watching my brother as well, and he was arrested two months later for a number of charges. My brother developed a reputation as one of the biggest bond, and that's when he came up with a master plan of robbing a bank. He and several others robbed a bank. Yes, he robbed a bank, faked his own death and fled to another state and was on his way out of the country until one of his counter parts stayed behind in Illinois and they caught his ass, and he started snitching on everyone.

Six months have passed, and nothing has changed. Wanting to do better for myself and my children, realizing that my then husband did not want to leave the game behind, I left with the kids and the clothes we had, didn't fight, or take anything else with me. I just wanted out of the abusive relationship. I was mentally drained, physically unfit and knew it was over. I wasn't going to let my kids suffer from seeing me in such a rut, from a man we trusted to be the man of the house promised to take care of his family and uphold his marriage vows. Don't get me wrong it was all good until we started using and abusing money, drugs family and each other. Believe me it's not a myth, crime does not pay, you do the crime do the time behind bars. My mind was already trapped in that life I just didn't want anymore.

I did a clean break and just didn't look back anymore. The funny thing about it was he would always tell other woman wasn't no room for them to start a relationship with him or get there hopes to high because I wasn't going anywhere. I was his wife, and he already had his family, and for a minute he was right I tried two times before and I came right back. The third time I relied on God and kept on moving, got a divorce and didn't look back. It hurt like hell! I sat down and really weighed my life, not my options. It was between a peaceful life or living a stressful life. And it took me awhile to trust another man.

I Corinthians 2: [14] *The person without the Spirit does not accept the things that come from the Spirit of God but considers them foolishness and cannot understand them because they are discerned only through the Spirit.*

So fast forward to today, my brother is now serving 35 years and I'm divorced. So, you can imagine I've done it all. So, I'm far from putting up with the bull. I just want a man to love me for me and live a Christian life. This man (Jesse) I'm dating now seems to fit that category. Everyone has a past they wish they could take back. Hell, if we could turn things around, we wouldn't need God and we all know how much we need him. So once again I'm going to take it slow and have fun, see where this goes. We got past all that craziness, the weekend really ended up nice. It was now time for me to jump back on the highway headed home. As I was on the highway sitting back rolling to the music, I didn't call him.

It gave both of us some time to think about this past weekend. But I will call and let him know I made it home safely and that I really appreciated the hospitality and the intimacy, I needed that! It definitely loosened up a lot of tension we both experienced. I can understand all he is going through, but he assured me it would all be over to just hold and trust him. I talked to God and trust in him, they had been separated for over two years which led me to believe he's free except for the paperwork. I'm almost home, it's only a two-hour drive, and about time the music gets to bumping, and traffic moves swiftly at the same speed I'm home. I'll call Jesse when I'm settled in the house. Whoops I guess I was wrong because he must have timed the ride because he's calling me. Hey Jesse, how's it going? He says he was just checking to see if I made it safely, how sweet of him to check on me. I told him, I'm almost there, and I was going to call soon as I got in the house.

again for the big distraction from his soon-to-be-ex-wife. I told him don't worry about it. I just pray that God will help you get through this divorce. He says it's getting to be very expensive, which is sad he says he's done all he can to provide for his family, but it obviously wasn't enough because she wants more through this divorce. I told him to pray over the situation and let God control the rest. That's what I did when I was getting a divorce. I wanted to date but that ended soon as it started. No one was good enough at the time! Seemed like every man I met had issues, except this one. We seem to be so compatible, it was things I was thinking, that he would say first. I thought he was putting on a damn good act, but it wasn't, that was good. I felt like one blessed sister, he had some of the same qualities and I was into him, nice right, like I said I was blessed. I'm in this house alone again but I love peace. I can go do what I want to do and come home to my own privacy. Occasionally, I may want a glass of wine or a shot of vodka, pop in a romantic movie and just do me. Me and Jesse will talk later and every time we talk, we stay on the phone for hours like 8th graders you know when we're under the covers and the conversation gets so deep, we just don't want it to end until we fall asleep on the phone.

This relationship has been going strong for close to a year but there's one problem, his ex and this divorce is not finale and I'm wondering should I hold on because she has a habit of calling when she's in need and that must stop! We're going to have a long talk on our next date. Maybe I should have just kept on dating with other men till he was free but that's a risk, people lie so much on dating sites, I better just be careful. One thing in my life I do look up to is God. I'm nowhere near perfect but being locked up gave me a clearer perspective on life. God finds a way of having you to truly depend on him and that's what I do. I believe in moral values, not being used again, to get what I deserve as a good woman and if a man doesn't have the qualities as a man that you are looking for, you should push on.

pique your interest as a good man or not! I'm good with the relationship I'm in now. We finally set our next date and he's coming here, so I get a chance to ask what I need to know about his soon-to-be-ex-wife. I asked him what's up with that! He tells me he's been raising her kids since they were young, he still felt the need to help them, but I address she chose to leave and the kids aren't calling you, she is, and I guess you have a decision to make. Maybe you're not ready to date until everything is final.

Maybe I'm wasting my time, and I don't feel comfortable when you answer and were together. He said from now on he wouldn't answer and said he would speak to her about calling, he wanted our relationship to move forward and he's praying this divorce is soon to be over. Then we started talking about my bucket list. I hope everyone has one because you have got to do what you dream of doing before you die, so it's been a list for years and I'm not getting any younger. So, I said to Jesse, I might as well tell you what I got on there! 1st is to go on a cruise, 2nd is to ride on a plane even though I'm scared of heights I can say I did it. 3rd is to take a trip to Myrtle Beach, and 4th is to get married again to a wonderful man who God created just for me *(this one I didn't tell, I wanted him to know, after we were married, big surprise, he had already figured that out)*. Not too big of a bucket list in my late 40's, I believe all things are possible right!

We laughed because this list sounded easy to him, and he had already been on a cruise by himself. I don't know if I could have done that, but he said it gave him peace of mind and we all need some peace in our lives. The visit went great. I'm starting to wonder am I a rebound to make his ex-jealous or if he's relieving some tension and I don't know it? I don't want to let him know just how much I am falling for him; you know how we do it, women hold back don't let him know all your feelings right away give it some time. Date for a while and that's what we did. We do our usual texting back and forth and talk for hours in the evening. One night he said he had to ask me a question. I said OK, fire away cruise with him? I said, "Well let me think about it" just playing, yes, I'll go with you. That's on my bucket list.

He said I know and I'm willing to fulfill that list if you'll let me. Blew me away, after we hung up, I was too excited I'm doing the damn thang as I jumped up and down. He later told me where we were going, Cozumel Mexico. Okay, I know now that I need to start shopping now for bathing suits and thongs. This really will allow me to see how he acts around other women; will he respect me or show his ass. This will let me know if I need to continue this relationship because we're past dating we're in a relationship.

I won't stand for no bull from a man, no more drama for me, I'm looking for something real and men say women bring the drama, no I've seen it all! I even had a stalker before the name even became legal. A guy I was dating would sit up at my job, sitting on the corner when I put my kids on the bus calling my phone constantly. I had to put a restraining order on this man to get him away from me and he was the one that got caught cheating. I just happened to be in the mall, me, and my niece.

My niece looks in hallmark store and there he was with another woman. I looked and was like what! I had a decision to make right then and there, should I walk away or confront him? Uh I'm a strong black woman I'll be damn if I just walk away. I looked at my niece and said watch this coward!!!! I walked up behind him and smiled at the young lady he was with. She seen me behind him so she smiled which triggered him to turn around, I said "Boo", you should have seen the sick look on his face like he had been up smoking crack all night.

He says Hi! I said hi, didn't know you were coming to the mall. I would have had you pick me up something, usually we shop together. The young woman said aren't you going to introduce us? I said yeah introduce us, he was shocked I reached out my hand and said I'm Othea the one he's been dating, she said you told me laughing. I said if he lied to you at the beginning what does that tell you. I told him I'll swing by your house and drop your key off in the mailbox. Then I looked back, said God always allows me to see a dog early so I don't make a mistake later. Believe it or not men hate rejection and for women to make them look less than, so he hurried made an excuse and dropped her off within that hour, because he was calling me, but I didn't answer. Twenty minutes he was knocking at the door. I didn't answer and told him if he didn't leave off my porch, I'd be calling the police. He got mad and left but it didn't stop there. He started stalking me till I got that restraining order on his ass.

Proverbs 28: [26] *Those who trust in themselves are fools, but those who walk in wisdom are kept safe.*

Dating was a serious no-no at the time, besides it was all about me and my kids and that's all I needed at the time, so I was doing me for a while until this relationship. I mean I've had a few compliments, but I like a humble man, I don't need a boastful man. And I seen a humble man in the one I'm dating now. So, I'm ready for this cruise, 4 weeks left, and he's paid for everything and made all the arrangements for us to have a great time and if nothing goes right that's one thing off my bucket list.

But the way we have fun it'll be alright. It's going to be a long drive to New Orleans to board the cruise ship, but I will enjoy experiencing New Orleans for the first time. I really need to start saving some money just in case in Mexico I want to shop, I want to bring a souvenir home. My kids are kind of skeptical, like mom you are going on a cruise, you don't even know this man, you just met him. Kids are always overprotective over there mother especially boys, the shit we've been through even if it was their daddy, no man is eliminated when they're doing wrong.

I've taught all three of my boys to treat women like you would treat me, that means never argue with them, walk away, don't ever raise your hands to hit them, never call them out of their name, and they do just that, and if you have children teach them the same morals and values I taught you. I don't mind my children being open enough with me to ask those questions. Who wants to see their mother go through any more abuse. And besides any signs I see leading up to abuse or neglect I won't stay around for!

You know it's exhausting planning and shopping for a cruise but at least I'll be ready for it, and everything is included, all you can eat all night. Time is flying, a week left before the cruise because we're driving to New Orleans which is a pretty nice ride so we will have time to site see, talk to get to know each other even better just look forward to a good time. The time has come, and we leave out in the morning. I'm just excited to experience this cruise!

So, he asked did we want to just grab a bite to eat, relax and rest for the long ride to New Orleans. We had a relaxing rest, got up early and left out at 6:00 am, stopped got a couple of Egg McMuffins and orange juice, cranked up the music and rolled out. We figured we'd stop in Memphis for lunch since they have the best barbecue restaurants there. We finally got there, got something to eat enjoyed each other's company then he kind of shared a little bit about his military experience, when he joined the Coast Guard. He experienced so much for the first time; he said their family had to appreciate everything they got because they had less than other children.

When joining the Coast Guard, he was able to sleep in a bed by himself and not wear the same clothing multiple times a week. He said he even wore a shirt the next day to school that his brother wore and got a spaghetti stain on the prior day. He said he remembered that, and when he got older, he would do all he could to not ever have to experience that again! He said he appreciated how hard his mother worked and all she sacrificed to give him and his sibling all she could, and he never had a bad thing to say about his mother whom he adored and misses her very much. Often tearing up when he speaks of her. That is one of the things I love about him, is his relationship with his mother, and how he speaks of her, you can really tell how much he loves her as she (his mother) passed away in 2001. My mother worked hard as well. She worked 2 jobs providing for a family of 11 yeah!

Big family and we had our moments we also slept together in the same bed at least 2 sisters in each bed and 2 brothers in each bed and so on. My older sisters passed their old clothes down to us because clothes never really went out of style, at least back then, so we had something else in common, to work and did not want for

New Orleans, we wanted to make sure we got there before the sun went down. I am in fear of being on the highway at night, as a result of a bad accident me and a few of my friends were involved in. My girlfriends and I were on the highway coming from a club, and one of my friends had an argument with her baby daddy about being in the club talking to another woman.

He didn't care because he got on the highway after the club was closing and taking that other woman home with him. My friend thought she saw the car her baby daddy and this girl was in and proceeded to chase him while we were in the car. We kept telling her slow down, it was raining we could barely see, and she kept on cursing saying she was going to catch up with him and whoop the lady's ass. We were like wait a minute why are you going to fight the woman, check your so-called man.

When men do this in your face, it's obvious they don't care what you think. In the past, I had to learn that the hard way, but she kept speeding. All of the sudden, she noticed lights in front of her and tried to brake, we started sliding and did a doughnut in the middle of the highway and slid into a ditch. I was terrified, my life had flashed before my eyes, and I saw lights everywhere. After that my girlfriend in the front had busted her forehead on the dash, I was just devastated and when we tried to open the door to get out the car, door was stuck because the way we were sitting in the ditch.

The police came and had to help us out of the car. I was just in shock, I started screaming look what you caused over some bullshit. The police questioned her, made her take a sobriety test, and luckily, she doesn't drink, so she passed the test. A few other friends seen the car in the ditch and pulled over to make sure we were alright. They arrested my friend who was driving, my other girlfriend got transported to the hospital to get stitches, and a friend that pulled over offered to take me home.

vision isn't too good either, so I avoid it if I can, and he respects that, and I appreciate it. We're almost there but were going across this bridge and it's so low that I can see the water, like its right up under the cement under the bridge and it was long like we never were going to get off. I asked him what bridge we were on, and he said 1-10 bridges going over Lake Pontchartrain which I wish would end quickly.

We finally get off there and he starts telling me about his experience in New Orleans when he was stationed there in the military for a few years. He knew the town quite well, where he stayed with his first wife and kids when he wasn't on the base for duty. He said people were really different there and weird. It was a lot of sinning going on there, people practiced voodoo, which was creepy, and he said he wanted to show me one thing for sure once we got closer into town that really would feel creepy. I was just happy to get there before dark.

He also alarmed me that an old song was real for New Orleans I said what's that, he starts to sing, The Freaks Come Out at Night!!!!! We had a good laugh with that. He suggested we check into our room, get something to eat, and maybe see a little bit of Bourbon Street. He tells me he had a surprise and wanted to show me something. I said cool I'm excited just to visit, so I asked him what did you want me to see? We drive to the surprise, and he, said were almost there brace yourself, he said no better yet close your eyes. I said oh a nice surprise I love surprises. It feels like he's turning right then he says open your eyes and I open them, and I say WHAT THE HELL!!!!!!! IS THIS REAL? MY EYES GOT SO BIG; it was coffins at a cemetery above ground. I said yeah now I'm totally creeped out. Why is this like this? He said it floods here and New Orleans sits below sea level, so they don't burry coffins, okay get me out of here!!

We proceeded to the hotel, we pulled up in this back alley, but he said the hotel is through here and it was. It was old-fashioned but nice and very close to Bourbon Street. We checked eat. He starts taking things out of his pockets and changing his shoes from the dress shoes he had on to gym shoes. I said should I change he said no but lock your purse up here as I'm doing with my wallet. I'm just taking cash, he said people here will snatch purses cut your wallet out of your pocket before you know it you've been robbed, and they definitely look for tourists and spot them miles away.

You must be extra aware of your surroundings. He said he worked in that area (riverside) for Mardi Gras for security and he said it was a lot of tourists scammed robbed taken advantage of when they're drunk. He said some thieves sit back and study how to rob innocent people on a regular basis, that was their lively hood, long as they didn't get caught. So now I'm more informed and look at him and say well I'm glad I got you on my side. And I tell him I would like some real gumbo he says I know just the place.

On our way to the restaurant, he says, look at that. There was a bank bag lying on the ground, as if someone had just taken the money out and through it down. We see what looks like a discarded wallet, and he says see that's what I was talking about.

As we began to stroll down the famous Bourbon Street in New Orleans to get something to eat and take in the sites, these two women (we believe to be Lesbians, by their mannerisms and speech) engaged us (mainly me) asking if I wanted to join them for a *%@#$ me silly shot. I said no, however, they began to get aggressive and began pulling my arm and insisting that I come with them. Jesse had enough and louder and angrier than I had seen him, yelled at them saying, she said no as he grabbed my arm from them, and we went on our way.

We get to the restaurant; the atmosphere is packed with people, nice loud jazzy music, and you sit yourself. I'm excited about New Orleans, past the voodoo, I've calmed down. I just want to eat some gumbo and enjoy this night. We will board the cruise

We proceeded to order, and he ordered some crawfish, it looked like a baby crab, some kind of red bug. He kept asking me to try it. Now I'll try just about any new food except for the ones staring back at me. I'm good, I'll watch him suck that down. The meal was good and very filling, and I noticed everywhere we eat or every store we go into before he receives the bill, he always asked do they have military discount? I'm like okay does this mean is he trying to be cheap or what? The funny part is a lot of places honored military discount. No wonder my dad used to say, I shouldn't have to pay for anything I served my country, I fought in the war. My dad didn't drive but when he took the bus he would get on the bus and just start walking to the back to sit down. The bus driver would say hey, the fare is 50 cents, he would look and say I'm not paying, I served my country.

The bus driver would say you're going to have to exit the bus if you don't pay the fare. My dad would say put me off, and some people would feel sorry or just didn't want to see the drama that was going to happen so they would pay the fare. I know this for a fact because I would be sitting there right with him embarrassed as hell! And the reason he doesn't have his car anymore is because the Centennial bridge had a 25cents toll you have to pay to get from Illinois side to Iowa side, my dad would get right up by the toll, act like he dropped the money and speed off and it was always someone sitting inside the toll booth to give change or make sure you paid but they had something better in mind for my dad not paying.

About time he got to the other end of the bridge there the Davenport police was waiting on him. Unfortunately, he had done this many times before, so they knew exactly who he was. They stopped us, called him by name and said why do you continue to do this? He stated I paid my dues to this government. I was in the back seat, my brother in the front leaned up and looked at the officer I said I'll pay it for my dad. The officer looked and felt say all of that to say I honor the military.

My grandmother had 17 children and I bet half served in the military, my daddy always said get you a military man. I guess it's happening. We had a great time that night eating and listening to music dancing, but he knew our limits, so it was time to get back, rest and jump on that cruise ship tomorrow. I could hardly sleep. I took out my clothes and ironed them that night took a shower well, not by myself. He snuck in on me pulling the curtain back asking can I come in with his finger in his mouth like a baby, my look was really! I gave in, yeah of course you know the rest if you don't, use your imagination. We got out, rubbed each other's back down with lotion and slept peacefully as we could hear others in the hotel still partying, happy to be in New Orleans. We woke up got dressed had a nice early breakfast. We didn't have to start boarding the cruise ship until 12:00 noon, so we also had time to walk down Canal Street for a couple of hours and shop a little and go sightseeing. He assured me we didn't have to eat but he eats every two hours it seems like. We stopped and got chicken at the famous Popeyes.

After eating, we got in our car and headed to the parking garage to park and get on the cruise ship. Just getting into the parking garage was a nightmare. It was so much traffic! We finally got up a ramp and I couldn't believe my eyes. Close up the ship was crazy huge. Damn, scared me because for one, I'm scared of heights, too, how is this huge ass ship sailing in the water? My eyes were so big. He said he wanted to take a picture; it looked like I had just seen a ghost. We laughed; he was happy I was excited.

[8] *For the sake of my family and friends,*
I will say, "Peace be within you."

We went through the process of checking in, took a picture from the cruise director and boarded. Boy my heart was racing, so many people laughing, drinking partying, having a good time. Hostess were running around serving these drinks with umbrellas in them, walking up to everyone. Jesse had to use the bathroom and while he was gone, this Hawaiian gentleman came up to me with a plater full of drinks, all different colors, all kinds with fruit in them and asked would I like one, I said sure he said OK what's your cabin number. I told him, he handed me the drinks and I tasted mine; it was good. When Jesse came back from the bathroom, he gave me a strange look.

I said look honey this guy gave me free drinks. He laughed; I said what are you laughing for? He said did he ask for your cabin number. I said yes, he said baby, alcoholic drinks are not free, but the food and entertainment are. I said what!!!!!! Really those two drinks cost? Jesse said yes, $8 each. He said that's ok. Now you know I said this drink better have me tipsy for $8 dollars. The ship was beautiful, it was food everywhere 24/7, we weren't going to be hungry that's for sure.

We didn't want to go to the cabin, he said till the ship took off and started sailing. We walked around, and looked at everything, just about everything you could do on land, you could do on this ship. This is crazy fun, and I'm checking off one of my bucket list items to boot. This is really happening. For a man to reach out and show compassion and fulfill this for me meant a lot. That speaks volumes! So far, so good, and on top of that we were having fun together.

We finally go to the cabin, but he notices our luggage hasn't come yet, they sit it outside your door he said when it animal made out of towels on the bed it was just so nice. Over the intercom they announced that every deck (that's what they call floor on a ship) had to go to a certain area of the ship for an emergency drill. He says this is standard, they go over what we would have to do in case we had to abandon ship. We left out to do that, it was quite a bit of people on each deck. We had to go to our designated area for the drill. These drills are to help prepare us if something happened to the ship, we'd know how to basically survive, board the lifeboat.

Hell, I looked at him, and asked, "has this ever happened"? He said no but they have to do this drill just in case. I said you were in the Coast Guard right you going to put that to use right. He said I'll make sure I save you. That was sweet. Some be like hell every man for themselves. So, after the drill we went back to the cabin and our luggage was there so that was good, we wanted to change into something comfortable, eat dinner and enjoy some kind of entertainment. We took out our clothes and prepared for a shower. I told him he could go first, nope he said ladies always first. I took off my shoes sat on the bed to take off my clothes to a little help along the way. So, we went back out on the deck dressed for the night and the sun was setting.

It was about 80% set, and beautiful. We ate first at a nice restaurant, and he asked if I wanted to go dancing, I said yes that's sounds fun. We walked into this loud club with a mixture of music young and old. The music we knew and jammed too was old school. I drank a few drinks; it only took 2 for me to get drunk and freaky. He seems to love the wild side of me. We went back to the cabin at around 1:00 am. Something about sleeping on water felt like cotton, I didn't get seasick not once!!! The next day we had a big excursion to go on the beach in Cozumel Mexico. I had packed 3 swimming suits I hadn't worn since I worked at the YMCA, teaching water aerobics to older people, and my own preschool classroom swam two days a week, so it's been years and I've gotten past a size 12, still got hips, ass and nice size breast, so I'm but I could lose a few pounds.

Proverbs 14: ³⁰ A heart at peace gives life to the body, but envy rots the bones.

So, we pull into the port of Cozumel Mexico and get on a bus provided by the ship for our excursion to the beach, all food, festivities, and drinks included. I'm so excited, however, but something felt strange I kept feeling someone staring at me. I looked around and it was this big black girl staring and she didn't stop. After a while of her staring, and she seen me staring back, she leaned over and told her friend, what sound like "I'm going to take her man." She looked me up and down as we got off the bus. I leaned over and whispered to Jesse, you got some secret admirers, he laughed and said who? I said those two big women over there, especially the real dark one with the big black hat and spray colored red hair. She looked like a dark Rasputia *(a reference from the 2007 movie "Norbit" starring Eddie Murphy).*

Literally, I shouldn't talk I just spoke about my weight, but I didn't do anything to make her even look crazy sideways at me, like I wasn't good enough for him. He laughed it off and we walked to the beach and went into separate dressing rooms to get changed into our bathing suits. I noticed while I was taking off my shoes a Mexican guy walked in, I looked startled, but he immediately walked back out. After I finished changing, I started looking for Jesse. He was around the corner, and I asked him where we put our other clothes. He said why didn't you get a locker, so I said let's go back to the ladies dressing room and I'll get one. We walked back around the corner to go in, and he said "did you go in here"? I said yes why, he said this is the men's dressing room. I said what, he laughed so hard he said male is spelled in Spanish. I said no wonder that man looked and ran out. He asked, did he see much? I said no, I was just getting my shoes off and no one else came in.

the men's dressing room changing. They probably got a kick out of that! Oh well, can't take away our joy let the fun begin. We walked out to the beach, it's about 90 degrees here in Cozumel Mexico, wind blowing lightly, and the sun is beaming. It's been about two hours now since we first got here, definitely have a tan but that didn't stop us. We are really enjoying each other and the atmosphere. We found some lounge chairs, put our towels on them. He wanted me to get in the water with him, but he made sure I put on these water shoes we bought, not knowing what that meant until I got into the water, looked down and started screaming.

I saw fish swimming around me. I started stepping on coral, algae, rocks seaweed around me and he said calm down those are just Minos swimming around you. He came over and held me tight and said I got you. They're more scared of you than you are of them. That was sweet, he kissed me softly on the lips then we heard this big splash and it was Rasputia *(never knew her name, I just gave her that name because she reminded me of that character in the movie Norbit)*. jumped in the water to distract us from kissing then she swam around us like a big ass whale "oops" did I say that!

Then she had the nerve to come up for air, shaking that red weave all over the place which made the water turn colors and scare the Minos away. I turned my head away and laughed to myself and told him you better control your girl he said that ain't my girl. I thought my girl was standing right here next to me. Her friend stayed on the beach, she knew not to get that cheap weave wet, she just laughed from her view in one of the lounge chairs, which was just three chairs down from us, real close right! Well, she made a big scene in the water and started talking to this other couple who was in the water.

They were half drunk, and they had what looked like margaritas in their hands standing in the water. I guess she wanted to get some real attention, so she seen this big bouncy house on water with a slide. She said she was going to swim out there and saying just for children, but she clearly didn't see it, or didn't care. She told the couple she was going out there, just when the wife of the couple was getting ready to say it's not for adults that slide could only hold children, but her husband hit her and told her to "shhhhhhh", don't tell her. They clearly were waiting for the outcome. Rasputia swam out there, I looked and told Jesse, she's swimming out there once again to get your attention. He said she's swimming out there to do what? I guess get on that bouncy house slide, he said that can't hold her. I laughed I know right.

We got out of the water to dry off a little and looked back towards that bouncy house, and we noticed the few kids that were out there had jumped in the water, we looked again and suddenly, the bouncy house just started caving in and sinking. The kids started quickly swimming out of the way, we looked seen a hand come up as it was going down then we saw a rescue boat speed pass. I thought ok, they're going out there to rescue the kids nope, guess who they had in the boat on their way back towards us? It was Rasputia, she had caved in that kid's bouncy house and got stuck. The kids' parents called for the rescue! Rasputia was hanging over the side of the boat, that weave was drawn up so badly it looked like an old dish rag, and she was gasping for air.

The couple in the water laughed so hard they spilled their drinks, and I couldn't help but laugh, me and Jesse were in tears. I hadn't laughed so hard in years. She got out of the boat and the rescue team wanted to make sure she was alright. When she seen us laughing, she immediately started cursing the rescue team out like she didn't need any help! I said God takes care of fools too. We started getting hungry, the beach had a buffet and open bar, so we walked to get us something to eat and drink, laughing all the way there. I asked was he impressed by her actions? He looked at me like really! Stop it! Let's eat. I said this is fun and I need a drink. He got food for us, and I went to the open bar and got a frozen strawberry daiquiri.

go. In Mexico the liquor is no joke. No wonder people were saying they didn't have to do an adventure or an excursion they would just enjoy the drinks and Cozumel, now I get it. If you're not a drinker, you only need two but I'm good and tipsy to the fullest. Well, we have got to continue our excursion. We get ready to jump on these water slides, well at least he is. I'm not going to mess up my hair, my niece took too long to do it, so I brought all the items I needed to keep it looking that way!

We get over to a nice size slide with a pool at the bottom to slide into, he said let's slide, not me you go right ahead. I'm not getting my hair wet you see how your secret admires hair was after the beach seen. Little did I know I thought the stalker was done until I felt this shove, it was her trying to get to that slide racing behind Jesse once again for attention. He walks up the slide, first she smiling looking at his ass. When did a black woman start looking at men's asses? I'm too busy looking at a man's shoes and monitoring his conversation when I first get approached by a man!

He gets to the top of the slide. I stay at the bottom standing in the pool when he comes down so I can take some pictures. This slide was a curvy slide, so I got some pretty good pictures. Then we looked up to see that she was standing at the top of the slide asking her friend to take some pictures of her. Jesse slid down and met me at the pool. We looked up, and the park worker at the top of the slide told her it might be a problem! I know because she was arguing with him very loud saying I can fit on here what you mean? So, he didn't want to argue anymore so he let her slide, and we heard a big rumble.

The Mexican couple that was standing in the pool next to us, looked at us and said what was that noise? We looked, and the water was splashing off the slide from side to side, all we could really see was red water and something big coming fast. We all ran to get out of the pool before it hit the bottom. It was her!!!!!! The splash in the pool was so big it actually got me and him and the couple standing next to us wet. When we looked, and the whole chlorine water red. Y awl already know I was in tears laughing and Jesse too. The Mexican couple was talking in Spanish all I could make out was "Infierno No" which means "Hell No" unknowingly to us! We just quickly walked away.

I couldn't take anymore watching her set herself up for physical abuse and embarrassment. We only had an hour left before we got back on the bus to head back to the ship, so we wanted to shop at least buy something as a souvenir. American dollars meant a lot, every one dollar was more than the Mexican Peso. We finally made it back to the bus. Once we got our seat on the bus, Rasputia (name I gave her) finally boarded, looking like she had had a very rough day. Someone asked her, how did you enjoy your excursion? It was as if someone insulted her. She burst out with "you all saw me having to be rescued in that boat". It was all Jesse and I could do not to **laugh at her.**

I can't wait to get on the ship, take a hot shower, put on some clothes to eat, and enjoy the rest of the evening. Every evening, we get a special dinner at a beautiful restaurant. I look at the menu and try food I've never tried before. He's simple, he always says it may look good but that doesn't mean it tastes good. After dinner we would take a walk around the ship, watch the sun go down and take in a live comedy show then dance and finish off the night. He might get lucky if you know what I'm saying. Being on a cruise is like a whole other world outside your home. You meet all kinds of crazy people some sane some not! For the most part it is a nice getaway. The next morning we're back in New Orleans off the ship and on our way home.

As we began the ride home, Jesse said he wanted to make a stop, to show me something that I would find very inspirational. Now, I am looking at the time, and don't want to be on the road at night as I was involved in a bad accident with my friends while driving at night. Jesse assured me that we had time. So now, I'm wondering what it is that he wants so badly to show me. As we approached Memphis, he asked me if I had ever been to the

King Jr. was assassinated, and now is a museum. He then proceeded to tell me about his experience, when he first visited it and the impact it had on him, and he wanted me to have that experience. Now, I'm excited, as I have always respected Dr. Martin Luther King Jr. and heard all about the place where he was assassinated, and told myself one day, I would visit. Little did I know that I would meet someone who would make that happen for me. The moment has come, we are now here at the Loraine Motel, a place in history. The cars from that fateful day are still there. Unfortunately, unknowing us, it was closed, they were doing some work on it, so we couldn't go inside.

As a result, they allowed us to go to the second floor and look in the window of room 306, the room where Dr. Martin Luther King Jr. stayed the night before he was assassinated. If anyone has ever been to the Lorraine Motel, you know that no one is allowed on the balcony where Dr. King lay after being struck by an assassin's bullet. On this day, we were able to stand there, we were able to put our hands on the door. A wave of emotions came over both of us as we stood there, absorbing all the history this moment held. It was somewhat overwhelming. Now, back on the road, we both sat silent, still under the emotion of what we just experienced. We made it a point that we would come back to visit when the museum was open. Jesse was right, this was something that I would find inspirational, and I now understand the impact that he felt the first time and he shared with me. I now feel it, and it has had an impact on me. I thanked him for sharing that experience with me.

Colossians 3: [14] *And over all these virtues put on love, which binds them all together in perfect unity.*

Once we get to Jesse's home, I'll spend the night there then head home the next morning. I had a great time, and it was on my bucket list so one down! We have so much fun together. We finish each other's sentences and laugh all the time, and that's surely a relationship you want to be in. To be able to enjoy each other, become friends first. Just enjoying the sex and thinking everything else will follow in a relationship, it just does not work that way. It's more to it than that and I've been taught from the best. You see older is wiser. My grandmother played a big role in my life so did my oldest sister before she died. They showed me how to act like a woman and respect myself and believe me those talks and lessons paid off. I have been blessed along the way, I never just settled for a man with no goals, no desires to get married, just shacked up to reap the benefits nope!

Through it all I'm blessed for my ups and downs; it just makes you stronger and wiser to not make those mistakes again. Well almost to St. Louis about 20 minutes away from Jesse house and all we can think of is relaxing. He has a jacuzzi in his master bathroom. He might offer me a bath instead of a shower. I feel so good just being able to have experienced a cruise and New Orleans. I can't wait to see what's ahead in this relationship. The night went well just as I expected, and he even got up early to fix breakfast, something was good the night before.

It's a two-hour drive for me to get home from his house. Lots of good memories from the trip to reflect on during the drive to get me home smiling from ear to ear. Back to work it is! I don't have a problem with being a single African American working woman but the man I marry should also have his own. We're too found out in the last few weeks this man is humble, hardworking, Christian an instructor and now pursuing his doctorate which is great. He's had goals he succeeded in, and he is very physically active in men's over 50 softball. He's invited me to a tournament so I can't wait to see him play.

I'm excited I'm going to my first softball tournament with men playing. When I hear softball, I immediately think of women softball teams. Oh well you learn something new every day. The tournament is in Indiana. I'm ready to start traveling I'm at that age now where kids are grown and on their own. God did bless me with 3 boys 1 girl they have successfully graduated all have jobs and doing fairly well with their own families. They call when they need to talk or about the grandkids yes, I'm a grandmother but they are demanded to call me NANA! Today is Wednesday and we've talked every day since the cruise.

Me and my long-distance boyfriend. Since I left his home, we talk so long I fall asleep on the phone. One night, I asked him if he wouldn't mind praying. He says he is a Christian, so he shouldn't mind praying for us. He said sure, I'll pray. It's a good thing when you have someone who can and is willing to pray. I know I have someone who will pray for me when I am unable to pray for myself. We agreed to pray before we hung up each night but. When he prayed, his voice was so soothing, I would fall asleep, and I would wake when he said Amen loudly so we could hang up the phone together. I adore a man who knows and has faith in God. I'm going to start packing today.

He'll be here Friday after I get off and will be spending another weekend together, but this time in Indiana. I'm excited also to see how he acts around some of his boys, especially since were in this new relationship! It's a 4-hour drive before we make to Indiana and were on our way as soon as he picked me up. We haven't stopped talking yet about our kids, grandkids and our up bringing. We have the same moral values, which is a very good insight into our new relationship. After a few stops we made it to food, but I'm fine with the fact that you can't even tell where the food he eats is going, he is very active. I'm amazed by this sport; it is over 10 teams here all men playing softball over 50 years of age. And from what I've seen this far my boyfriend starts every game, he is just that good. The weekend just got started so I'm here to enjoy plus relax.

The room we checked into its nice and he's still that respectable man around his friends and that is a plus. I've watched two games and starving never knew these men could play so long. We will get something to eat, take it back to the room shower and be up early in the morning for a game that starts at 8:00 am. That means **no fooling around** tonight, just rest. Why do black women get up two hours early? Probably because our makeup and hair take the longest. It's nice to see black women going natural, it shows strength, faith, power, and courage. I'm all about that. Wow first tournament, and I am so excited.

I was sitting in the bleachers like a little kid, and one of Jesse's teammates started talking to me. He asked me who was I there to see, and I told him I was with Jesse, and he said, oh, he's a good guy. Have you ever seen him play? I said no, he said, so you never seen him run, or hit? Again, I said no, he said he sounds like a horse when he runs. I said, like a horse. Get out of here, he said, no I'm serious, watch him when he runs. Sure enough, Jesse came up to bat and hit a ball in the gap between two outfielders and he was off and running. His team mate said see what I tell you. They won, and he's very happy I came to support him. We're going to the room shower and go celebrate with a victory dinner rest up and travel home in the morning.

Matthew 5: [37] All you need to say is simply 'Yes' or 'No'; anything beyond this comes from the evil one.

Six months later and we've been going strong in this long-distance relationship, who says long distance relationships don't work? It definitely depends on who you date, but after a year if you have not made no real commitment, I'm gone! I've been teaching children for over 20 years, and I truly enjoy it but the business I work for is closing. There program and my job are on the line so me and Jesse have been talking about me moving there where he says, there's plenty of jobs and he loves our relationship, so I've been online applying for a lot of jobs, and I have three interviews, so things seem to be falling in place. My kids are grown, they have their own families and I need to start doing for me, at least to be happy and that, I am at least, for now I am. It's December my job closed, and we've decided to move in together. I support him and he supports me. I'm packed and have been for two weeks now.

I'll be moving on the first of the year for a new start. We're renting a U-Haul and I'm moving to Shiloh, IL. I've decided to rent my home out and receive a little extra income to help with bills and hopefully I get hired at one of these jobs. You never know how much you have until you get ready to move. He has a 4-bedroom house and full basement. I will put my stuff in the basement until we can go through all of this and rearrange this house the way I like it. This home has his ex's creative style and it's too much of memories. I'm tired, we moved all this by ourselves, and my feet hurt and I'm starving, so all we want to do is eat and sleep.

It's been 10 months and time is winding down. I've started working and things are going well, and I mean well! Holidays are coming and we have asked all our kids to come down for Thanksgiving. It's a four-hour drive from Rock Island where my have plenty of energy, they'll be fine. Jesse's kids are further away, Texas and North Carolina, and we're not able to make it. Thanksgiving was great, this gave Jesse and the kids an opportunity to get to know each other more intimately. Jesse already knew I wasn't going to go past a year without being married so he shared with my kids his intentions to get married and treat me like the queen he says I am.

The only one that had a lot of questions was my youngest De'Mar. He's overprotected of his mother only because of the heartache he had to endure inside my belly those 9 months from dealing with his dad. It is true the whole time I was pregnant with him I hated his father and De'Mar came out looking just like him. He denied De'Mar because of his own indiscretions of cheating with another woman and we were pregnant at the same time. He was there when her baby was born but wasn't there for the birth of De'Mar. Let's just say I laid there for a day before anyone showed up. Funny how things work out though. We never did make it work and divorced and yes it affected my child.

It took De'Mar a long time to even respect his father let alone speak to him. So, I can see De'Mar always being overprotective. Jesse is a good man, and we have a great understanding spiritually as well as physically, we don't want a big wedding, and a lot of people. We're okay with a judge in front of us. Yes, a courthouse wedding and just us to celebrate. We're too old and set strictly on being happy and living in Gods commandments.

Genesis 2: [24] That is why a man leaves his father and mother and is united to his wife, and they become one flesh.

Wow it's been three years since we have been married some our families have been distant from us since we've gotten married but that's fine, we enjoy each other, and we didn't need family's approval to get married. We have a few bumps in the road Jesse busy teaching and me busy working and I volunteer at the hospital near me. I enjoy helping people, I don't know why but I've always been this way and it's a great thing to care for others. Me and Jesse decided to get our grandkids this summer, all of our kids live distance away, so we want to be able to spend some time with our grandkids to let them know Papa and Nana love them and were always there for them.

So, we got this plan, that the parents bring the kids all the way to our home and drop them off for two weeks and they agreed. Jesse had to meet his daughter halfway to Texas for her kids. It didn't work out for his sons' kids in North Carolina. What parent you know wouldn't want to drop their kids off for two weeks. They can take a vacation and not have to worry about their kids. In addition to all this, I'm planning a surprise party for Jesse. It's his birthday and it fell on Father's Day. I've been planning this for months and some of his softball teammates have been helping me. I hope he's surprised, and things go well. He deserves it, he's been working hard.

The day has finally come. Wow everything is going well, and Jesse's coach Ronnie rode with him to the house for me, to distract him. We all hid in the garage so when he opened the door it was a big surprise. Family and friends. What more could you ask for having a good time barbecuing drinking and you know we got to have a spades game going. I'm a mess when it comes to competing in spades, I must win everything I can't let no one beat bragged how good he was so I couldn't wait to get him on the table even though his brother-in-law Sean from another marriage said he couldn't be beaten. It's all out fun. After I send them home as losers. The party is going well, I need to see my kids off and let my grandkids kiss their parents' good-bye. The grandkids will be with us for two weeks, people keep calling us crazy, 10 kids in the house. I have a plan that should work and will have lots of fun. We have a big enough house to accommodate all. I'm going to put these kids to work, now that everyone's gone. Get sleeping arrangements under control, give them a snack before bed and then the lights go out. I refused to take any grandchild that wasn't potty trained. I didn't have time to change diapers. I wanted the kids to be able to dress themselves so we could get up and go. You should've seen how fast the parents skirted out of the driveway. I don't know if they planned a vacation or not, but they better appreciate the break from their kids.

I Peter 5: [5] In the same way, you who are younger, submit yourselves to your elders. All of you, clothe yourselves with humility toward one another, because, "God opposes the proud but shows favor to the humble."

We had with us three grandkids from Texas and seven from Rock Island. Crazy right. Yeah, I had the majority this time, but we love them all the same. They're going to help clean, and the girls are going to learn how to cook. They're going to act like kids here, not taking care of each other, letting us take care of them! We sometimes place our kids in a position where the oldest child must take care of the youngest. It gets so bad, we put a lot of responsibility on the oldest and expect them to do our work as well. It's been a week of fixing 3 meals a day for 10 kids, that does not include baths, washing clothes etc. It's draining. About the time we get through and ready for bed its 10:30pm when me and Jesse hit that bed were out, but I feel as a woman I do most of the directing. I even got mad because I felt Jesse wasn't helping me enough with the kids, but there is no way I could have done all of this on my own. All I can think of is one more week. And making sure these parents meet us at the halfway point. I wasn't so sure that my youngest son De'Mar's daughter would make it.

She was only three at the time, but she was potty trained, and he assured me she was very smart for her age and that's his only child for now. It's so much to do in the St. Louis metropolitan area, which includes both sides of the Mississippi River, Missouri and Illinois. I had two weeks planned plus Jesse's softball tournaments. We will stayed busy. One thing my grandkids will remember about NaNa and PaPa is that we love them, and they can always come here and spend time with us. Both of us being teachers, well Jesse, a professor teaching college student, and me preschool. It gives our grandkids the incentive to accomplish and tomorrow I must meet our daughter in Lincoln, the halfway point (two-hour drive) to drop off seven of our grandkids.

Then two days later we must meet our other daughter at the halfway point from Texas for the other three grandkids. The gas and travel are expensive, but we will sacrifice anything for our kids. Finally, we are back home alone, no grandkids. Wow I think we've slept two days straight. We were so worn out for those two weeks; I think we got up to eat, shower and got right back in the bed. I don't know if we're cut out to do a whole two weeks. We will have to break it down to maybe a week. Well, kids are doing ok, everyone's working, and grandkids are a year older. My mother is doing well, still works for the school district at the age of 80 and that tells me don't give up, keep moving. My mom has always said that because some people retire, sit around, and do nothing then wither away.

Genesis 4: Adam made love to his wife Eve, and she became pregnant and gave birth to Cain. She said, "With the help of the LORD I have brought forth[j] a man."

So back to reality working and taking care of us. Jesse spends most of his day in his office on the computer. When he is not teaching on the weekends, he also teaches on-line classes. And because he is so passionate about it and wants to do the best for his students, it takes up a lot of time, even from me. But I'll be patient and wait to see if he notices me. In a relationship as long as the man is true to his words, we should be supportive and be patient with them. Besides always stay focused on your own goals and don't ever depend on your spouse to dream them for you. God gives us a gift we should pursue because he wants us to prosper. The summer is almost over, and fall is coming and that's my favorite time of the year.

I'm a jean and boot kind of girl. I have the shape like most black women to rock in any style of jeans with my nice hips, round luscious butt, and boobs just right. I'm good as they say. We decided to travel back to Rock Island to see my mom, she hasn't been feeling too well and the last thing I want is for something to happen to my mom. I'll bring her to Shiloh before I let any illness get out of hand and take my mom. We always said our mother will never go into a nursing home, and with 11 kids, it shouldn't be a problem. It's a four-hour drive back home but me and Jesse laugh and talk so much we barely feel the long ride when we go. We usually stay one day, (I dislike that city even though I grew up there) I've always had bad memories from being bullied in school, addiction, imprisonment, and divorce.

Every time I get close, pulling off that exit into town I feel a great darkness come over me. I left for 10 years moved back, and couldn't last a couple of years there, it felt like I was doomed like it wasn't going anywhere. The men didn't have the same goals I had, and they wanted to stay in Rock Island and never move and go anywhere. For that day I would make my rounds visiting everyone then get up early and leave the next morning, that's how quick it was.

The older I got the messier and more distant my family got. The distance from one another was because of grudges, jealousy, whatever you could think of that was us. Our family has been through a lot with the crack epidemic in the 90s so we do not dare allow one of our children to sell or use drugs but the family we have is so big someone is bound to make that mistake, and definitely learn it will cost them a world of troubles. That's why my brother has already done over 15 years of prison time. He went in early in his 20s and still currently there. I wrote President Obama for him to have an early release but that didn't work because there was another charge that came into play. I never trusted my brothers' two sons that my mother raised. They were spoiled, always in trouble, and very disrespectful up until this day. I think in a large family there's always going to be some drama.

They are my nephews. I never liked my boys hanging around them. They were always up to no good. One doing prison time as we speak for his third time and the other ones been in and out of the county jail so much, he pays lawyers just to stay out of the jail. My son De'Mar tells me we're too hard on them and he's always trying to see the good in them. I just don't see it; all I see is disrespect from cursing out their grandmother (my mother) who raised and spoiled them. Always' pulling a gun out and threatening to shoot someone, even one of their own aunts in the face.

But De'Mar still tried to see the best in them. He remained close, started music with them, and when you saw him, you seen his cousin (my nephew). They became the best of friends. I think De'Mar was his savior, he even told me one time that he felt sorry for him. Every time he got into a fight with his drunken stupor attitude, De'Mar was there to save him. All my children were calling my kids dumb.

Education plays a big part in life, it has a lot to do with where you were headed, it provides choices. I wanted the best for my kids, and they all graduated. Spirituality also played a big role in my life, and I wanted the same for my kids. And because of that, they were all baptized at a young age. They knew of and had a relationship with God. As a Sunday school teacher, and my relationship with God, worship, and interactions within the Church, I believe it had a positive influence on my kids. It is that relationship with God that got us through in good and bad times. But the older my children got they drifted away from church but still believed. I consistently prayed for them and went to church while they got grown and produced fruit with their own family. That's why I have all these grandkids and I encourage them to have a relationship with God. My daughter Sheena is a lot like me. We could never live together. Strong personalities together are not good. One or the other always wants to be in charge.

My oldest son Darwin is quiet in his own way, he plays the role of two characters. He's a rapper by night and a father, family-oriented man by day. He works hard and provides for his family. He doesn't allow his girlfriend to work, she's a true homemaker and mother. Every time she sets out to follow her gift, she never finishes the task she started. I don't know if that's Darwin pushing her to stay at home or she feels she'll fail. My middle son Rolando (Zay) is a lot like his father. He'll tell you quickly he's not, but there are so many similarities from the way they stand, speak and personalities. Especially when it comes to women. Rolando is the same astrology sign as mine. When we fall in love, we love hard, and loyalty is a must. I'm the best horoscope sign there is, yep you guessed it Aquarius.

It depends too around the time of your birthday because I've seen some mean ones but still loving and loyal. Zay is a good father, loves his children a lot, and spends a lot of time with them. His mind is focused on his kids, but he's got that baby mamma you either! I don't know how she justifies that, but in her mind it's right but it's insane too everybody else. Now my baby boy has been the one most emotional but is always looking for a great outcome. He's a great father, negotiator and hates to see someone bullied. He's always taking care of others and families he just adopts off the street. All I've ever heard is you have such a good and respectable son. He quickly says I take after my mother; he never says that about his dad. He despised him for denying him, but God seen fit to show the truth and there was a lot of hurt behind that situation. Come to find out that he is a splitting image of his dad. It was my child he did not want to claim imagine that!!!! Whenever I would get upset with one of the other kids, it would be De'Mar that would calm me down using his Christian faith on me. I'm just blessed, everyone is grown up and has a life of their own now.

Psalms 34: [18] The LORD is close to the brokenhearted and saves those who are crushed in spirit.

Everything seemed to be going great until my life took a devastating turn. One hot day in August just getting off the computer, tired as hell, I was on Indeed putting in applications for a new job. Every time I work somewhere I seem to be a threat to someone by my skill set, others lack of said skill set, so jealousy rears its ugly head, or they say I think I'm smarter than them, but hell a lot of these jobs I've done are common sense. A teaching job takes a lot of passion, patience, and compassion for children. I tell anyone if you can't walk in your place of employment happy with what you do, you don't need to be there! I hear a lot about this, if it wasn't for this check I wouldn't be here! My job cares nothing about state DCFS policies and procedures. They work their way around it just to get that private pay and federal government money, and grants from the state.

It's about 11:00pm and the phone rings. I look at the caller ID. Me and Jesse are still up so it's not a bother to answer it's my daughter on the other end shouting and screaming in the phone "mom there rushing De'Mar to the hospital." I'm trying to calm her down to hear what she's saying until I heard the words "he's been shot!" All I remember is Jesse picking me up off the floor. I must have fainted or went into some type of shock. I started screaming, asking, "was it true"? All I kept saying is we need to go. I didn't grab anything, just started running for the door till he stopped me again and said we need to get dressed, grab our purse wallets and leave. I just kept screaming God please I've done everything you asked. You promised to answer my prayers, You promised to keep my kids safe. We grab the essentials and jump in the car. I was shouting to Jesse to hurry up not even thinking it was 11:30 pm at night and 4 hours away. All I can remember is I

God begging please save him, save my baby. We were on the road, I started calling my family, first my mom waking her up asking her to go to the hospital see what's going on. She immediately said she was getting up and on her way. The hospital emergency room called Jesse's phone and ask how far out we were, we were we on our way he spoke to them and hung up the phone. You see what's nerve wrecking is I never get on the highway at night. I had a bad experience in my younger days being out with some friends, and now I have bad vision at night, and I don't let anyone else drive me as well. But I think I was in a state of shock because I just needed to get there to my son. The drive was going too slow, and the phone kept ringing with different family members calling Jesse. He kept answering, I could not, I was to hysterical hollering at God putting me in this position. Jesse did assure me we were getting close. I didn't even realize I didn't have shoes on. He grabbed them for me and threw them in the back seat. He kept saying please put your shoes. I don't want you to cut your feet or hurt yourself.

Have you ever felt like you couldn't breathe? I was gasping for air and crying at the same time or was I having a panic attack? We were pulling in the hospital straight to the emergency we jumped out and ran straight for the emergency room we started looking around, and it was completely empty. We thought we were in the wrong place it was so quiet. We see a desk where a nurse was sitting, we ask her was there a young man brought in the emergency room she said yes, I gave her De'Mar name, and she told us to wait she was getting the doctors. Moments later two doctors came out and asked could we step in a side private room. The look on the doctor's face was a look of distress. One of the doctors said they did all they could do to save him. I screamed save who? They said De'Mar. I asked them to let me see him. They said that I could not see him. They said he was locked in an evidence bag for investigative purposes, because his death was suspected to be a murder and under investigation. I argued, "what do you mean I can't see my child?" I need to see if it's him. I remember hear them tell me I couldn't see him. I ran out of the room; I remember dropping to the floor beating my hand against the hard floor until Jesse seen blood and grabbed my hands. Jesse tried to get me off the floor but couldn't. By that time, my oldest son had arrived at the hospital, and he tried getting me off the floor, but to no avail, so Jesse just held me right there on the floor until I was ready to get up. It took what seemed like hours for me to get out of that hospital.

I believe I was still in shock. Every time I cried, I had a panic attack, like I couldn't breathe. They wanted to take me back to the hospital, I said No! All kinds of crazy thoughts were going through my head. Why me? Why my son? God, you couldn't just take me I screamed. God, You promised me if I prayed you would protect my family. My son was baptized, saved, he knew You, talked about You, served You by helping others. I was so devasted, is this a dream why can't I wake up? De'Mar did good deeds, he took care of an older woman who died at 108 years old. She always said De'Mar was going to be something special. He started volunteering at a retirement home at the age of 13.

I made him and my middle son Rolando, volunteer so they could learn how to appreciate the things they receive and for them to always show love towards others. During that time, he latched on to Mrs. Beatrice till she died. Why take good people who are serving You? All I needed was to hear back from God saying the reason He took my son? Jesse kept saying I should see a doctor, that was the furthest thing from my mind. A nurse rushed out with bandages and began wrapping my hands. My oldest son sat down on the floor and said, mom we must leave. I refused to go anywhere.

I was so out of breath from crying and screaming and a few anxiety attacks in between I started to dose off but would jump back up with that same anxiety attack. Is this I dream? Why don't I just wake up. I looked at my oldest son Darwin and asked, "did De'Mar die?" He said yes mom let's go home and get some rest. It that room one more time, you could barely hear a pen drop and there was no one in there but us. We got out to the parking lot it was like I was carrying a weight on my back and the further I walked away from the hospital the heavier it felt. We followed Darwin to his house, got out and went up to his Loft. My daughter in law was waiting at the door with her arms open wide. I looked around seeing De'Mars pictures on the wall, and it made me break down again and collapse in her arms.

They rushed me over to the couch and made sure I was ok and continued to say I needed some rest. There's not going to be any rest, every time I dosed off it was a nightmare shortly after, so sleep wasn't an option that night and it probably never will be. My head hurt so bad from thinking and crying and screaming, I had no energy for planning a funeral. Burying my baby was the furthest thing from my mind. I couldn't do it! It's around 5:00am. Hours have gone by; my phone rang nonstop from the time I left Shiloh till now. So many people leaving messages, I couldn't even look at the rest of my children.

I still had one daughter and two sons. It just kept going through my mind the pain he must have endured. I felt that if there were people around, why didn't they do anything to save my baby, why didn't God save my child? Darwin said mom we need to make some arrangements he needs a proper burial. I knew that, but I'm not understanding how my child dies before me. No that's not the way it works, we do not bury our children; children are supposed to bury their parents. I never felt so much pain. Darwin and his father had to be the ones to view his body at the funeral, there's no way I could've done that. I wanted to see my baby at the hospital, eyes open, that big smile on his face. To see him in a box, I just couldn't do that! Darwin came back a couple of hours later, they couldn't set a date for funeral arrangements without me, and they needed a down payment.

One thing that was very upsetting to me and my ex-husband was neither one of us kept life insurance on our children had a family of their own, we felt it was time that they got their own. It's unfortunate, but it is all too common within the black community, that we don't always keep life insurance.

I am not saying that black people don't have life insurance because a lot of us do, however, what I am saying is that it is common to see that we do not, especially the younger generation. I wish I had kept it on my son, or that he would have had it on himself, because the expenses were an extra stressor on top of our devasting loss, especially, as some family members you may look to for support are living check to check, and unable to support you financially. My daughter-in-law, LeAnn told me that she had heard of a GoFundMe account we could set up, in addition to having a fund raiser for people to donate, so she called around a few places on my behalf. De'Mar's job donated, and we greatly appreciated that heartfelt donation.

As anyone could imagine, I am devastated, out of my mind, and do not know where to turn. As a Christian, my faith was shaken to its core. I know someone reading this may say, as a Christian you should have leaned on God. I understand that, truly I do. At that time, I was so angry with God. Yes, you read that right. I was angry with God. How could God allow this to happen? Why? I was full of pain, disbelief, confusion, just to name a few of the emotions. I did not say I gave up on God, I said at that time I was angry and couldn't understand, didn't understand. I reached out to Churches, Pastors in the area, asking them to help me understand this.

Where do I go from here? How do I process this? De'Mar was well known in the community, and beyond that he was well loved. I was not the only one devastated by my son's death, his siblings, nieces, nephews, cousins, aunts, and uncles took it very hard as well, especially his sister, as they were always together, even working the same job together. His friends as well as the community were also devastated. Everyone was in disbelief, rocked to the core. His friends called for a candlelight vigil with he walked each day to visit his friends, the same street his sister and cousin lived on for years, and now sadly where he lost his life. I didn't want to go; my heart was shattered. I felt helpless thinking what else could I have done to save my child. All the people who lived in that area were being questioned and we hadn't heard anything yet.

The vigil started at 7:00 pm close to dusk. We had to go out and purchase candles. We figured we would go to a dollar store nearby but soon as I got out of the car a mass of people young and old started walking up and hugging me. Some were in tears telling me stories of how good De'Mar was to them. Every time I moved forward towards the store someone else was walking towards me. Some also handed me money to help with funeral arrangements. I never made it in the store, so my daughter-in-law came out saying they were sold out of candles. We had to search multiple stores to find some.

I grew up in this city and the city watched my children grow until we moved to a different city, but then the children wanted to move back home to be close to family. I remember moving to Virginia, but we ended up moving back after six months. The cost of living was expensive, and they wanted to put my two youngest back a grade in high school. The credits they had from Rock Island wouldn't transfer to Virginia. The education there is far more highly accredited than in Rock Island. I refused to hold my sons back, especially when they worked hard to get those credits. We rented a 16 ft. U-Haul packed up and drove back home to Rock Island, IL. I drove the truck and my middle son Rolando drove my car for about six hours until I couldn't take it anymore of him staying in the left lane going too slow. I eventually signaled for him to follow me. Once we pulled over in a gas station, of course he was hardheaded saying he got it.

I immediately grabbed the keys from him and told De'Mar to drive the rest of the way, which was about another 11 hours. De'Mar was a child with patience but also had that leadership trait.

candlelight vigil. When we got there, there were so many people there, I didn't know where to actually stand but when they saw me, they made it known they wanted me to be up front. It was a camera crew there from the evening news (channel 4). I allowed some Pastors to speak, I wanted to hear what was really on their mind and what are they going to do now to help this community due to gun violence!

Churches have changed so much. I remember growing up Pastors use to be out in the community talking to people on the streets about how God could save their lives. Now they don't step foot out of the church, yet they collect tithes and offerings for private jets, fancy cars, etc., and we wonder is the money for them or for God and His works. Actions speak louder than words! And of course, just like I thought, out of 4 Pastors only one actually spoke on the neighborhood, because her church was a half of a block away from where De'Mar died. She had such a great heartfelt message to everyone about death and coming together to save our children in that area, but she stated we all need to focus on these children's future and how can we do that inside the church.

After all the Pastor's had spoken, the news interviewed me, asking me what was De'Mar like. I shared with them that all they had to do was look around, he was well loved by so many, he gave and didn't expect anything in return. He always had a smile on his face, so you never knew what was going on inside because that smile shone brighter. They asked if I wanted to share anything with the community, what would I share. I said, if you are a mother who has lost a child, help me to understand, and if you are a Christian show me in God's word how to help me get through it.

I also shared I know someone knows what happened and who did it, and I have already forgiven you for what you have done. Once I spoke, my son Rolando hugged me, and that was all I could do. This was a very emotional candlelight vigil and it hurt standing right there in that area. So many wept at the loss and

and he stated him and De'Mar walked and talked all the time to the gas station. He said he had so many dreams of leaving and taking his gifts to other places in the world and to give his children everything a father could offer; he even spoke about God. The young man asked me how there can be a God who is a protector but couldn't stop all the evil that's done in this world. He said he didn't want to depend on God and be let down. He said he'll take his chances on himself.

That's what I've seen for the last two years of trying to get young adults to see the devil is lurking, roaming this earth, stealing killing and destroying through people. I was tired and ready to get away from an area where my son suffered. People started to leave after about two hours, others sat around and drank liquor and smoked weed. They didn't care who seen them, mainly young adults sat there all night.

The next day I wanted to go to the police station. I wanted to know who was in charge of my son's case and to meet the chief of police. As soon as I walked into the police station the assistant behind the front desk, looking at us as to say what do they want? Especially when you see three or more black people walking in anywhere at the same time. I asked to speak with the chief of police or the detectives working on De'Mars case. We were told to have a seat and wait; they would call and speak to one of the detectives. About 10 minutes later a detective came down to introduce himself and escorted us upstairs.

When I say us, I mean me my oldest son, my husband and De'Mar's father. I went right in to asking questions. The detective said he had just received the case and he was trying to piece together all the evidence he had, and he would start questioning people. I told him to get started while it's still fresh in people's mind. I didn't want to take up anymore of his time. I wanted to let him know I was a mother who wants justice for my son, and I will continue to meet with them and watch their progress. My children lived in that city, so whatever they hear from the community they because once there's another murder case, they move on to the next one as if they don't care. I refuse for my son to die in vain like another young black man gone!

Every time I thought about it, I asked God please wake me up from this nightmare, that didn't happen. What is going on in this world, why do bad things happen to good people like losing my sister from asthma, my brother from cancer. I could go on without a direct answer from God. De'Mar father called my oldest son and asked could we meet at my mother's house. I'm assuming he had already told Darwin what he wanted. I despised this man for so many reasons, mainly for not stepping up being a dad to his children. Whoever he was dating at the time, that's who he put before his kids. I had to go to his father for money for diapers, food, etc. Every time I saw him; I would embarrass him in front of whoever he was with for not taking care of his own kids.

Besides the simple fact De'Mar held a grudge for a while against him for not claiming him but before he died, he forgave him. Forgiveness is hard sometime and takes a while for some people including me. We are approaching my mom's house, and I see family members standing out front. I guess they figured since I never answered my phone, they knew I would eventually come there in that house. My momma raised 22 children there, so that was a meeting point when bad things happen to a family member.

There was one person I definitely did not want to see, my nephew I hated his actions, his behavior, the trouble he caused. We got out the car, and His dad (De'Mars father) was already there with his wife (but not the woman he cheated on me with) the one he did cheat on me with she tried to kill him. He wears a scar from his ear down to his neck to this day, as a result of her trying to kill him. Sometimes you do reap what you sow, and that scar is there for life like some of the scars in my life I endured from him. We went in and sat down. My mom asked how I was, I just said not good, I don't think I'll ever be the same. His dad, DeMar's started to talk about the arrangements and how much it would cost to bury he would, he was always taking care of someone else's kids rather than his own. Once my children started having kids, I encouraged them to get life insurance for their families. I will say to every parent who has young adults, keep the life insurance on them until you know they have it! The cost of $8000 dollars, and possibly more, depending on how extravagant you want to get, to bury a loved one.

The devastation of losing a loved one is enough stress, let alone the stress of trying to figure out how to pay for burying them, especially a child. We had to start putting our heads together to get this money and it wasn't going to be easy. So, it's going to take some fundraising to get my son buried, and my mind was not on that. So, my daughter-in-law LeeAnn took the lead and set up a GoFundMe me account and a fund raiser at Buffalo Wild Wings. We also received checks from churches, his friends, and people from his job, along with some cash that my husband and I had access to too, all of this was very helpful. This along with God's help, we were able to dress him and pay for everything. In addition to my son's family, his friends also felt the sting of his death, questioning why bad things happen to good people. Currently, I am devastated, and I definitely do not have an answer. I am still angry with God and looking for an answer for myself. The next day it was time to go home. The funeral wasn't for another week. I couldn't rest there and couldn't eat; I was always sick to my stomach. Jesse suggested we go home. Remember, we just left when we got the phone call, we didn't take time to pack for any length of time.

Revelations 21: [4] *'He will wipe every tear from their eyes. There will be no more death' or mourning or crying or pain, for the old order of things has passed away."*

The whole four hours on the highway home, I couldn't do anything but cry. Jesse thought with the peace and quiet at home it would be better, it was worse. The only one in our home is us. I didn't get phone calls from family or friends, if so, it was only for arrangements. In the most devastating time of my life, when I needed them most, my sisters, my brothers didn't call to check on me, didn't offer to help me. They figured Jesse was there and he would take care of me, which he did, the best way he could, but I needed my siblings, and they let me down. They were not there for me, and that hurt me on top of the pain I was feeling from the loss of my son. They went right back to living their lives, while I felt like I had no life to live. I was ready to give up, my mind was so screwed up, not knowing how to think mentally, and feeling lost, and abandoned by God spiritually. I needed some help, I needed to talk to someone, a psychiatrist a spiritual leader someone that this has happen too before, someone who can relate. My aunt called me, she wants to talk to me. Every time I go see someone, I immediately start crying so the conversation usually goes in one ear and out the other, but I'll go see her when I get time.

I'm looking for clothes to take back for the funeral. I don't even want to go back, but I know I must bury my baby boy. One of the hardest and most devastating things I ever had to face. I keep asking God why me? I can't get any sleep, and every time I doze off, I have a nightmare. So, I ease out of the bed not to wake up my husband. I go down to the kitchen, I walk around cleaning up but there's only so much cleaning you can do because eventually, you start wiping things over and over again. I tried not to think about it but all I could do was walk around the island screaming at God.

me until I got so tired, I dropped to the floor and scooted against the wall. My face is numb from crying, I'm so hurt, heartbroken, and angry at the same time. God, do we deserve all this violence? Constantly, day to day hurting each other. What demons are people facing? Theres is no way you pick up a gun and not know this weapon can end a person's life. You can just look at mass shootings how it takes several lives and is strategically planned out to kill many people. This world, this new millennium as they call it, they can't hash out their differences so one uses a gun to make you disappear forever.

What's our defense as parents? What do we do? How do we explain to my son's children your father isn't coming back anymore. Trying to get them to believe there is a heaven everyone is going to one day. Then that next question a child might ask, why did he go without saying goodbye or take me with him? What's our response? Our family had to step up immediately and help take care of his children. How will they deal with this funeral? Every time someone looks at his oldest child, they just shake their head and say those same words, she's a splitting image of her father. How long should I sit on this floor with this migraine that no pain pill will cure? I just happened to look over at the patio, the sun is coming up, so I've been down here for hours.

This past week I might have gotten 28 hours of sleep. Tears rolling down my face I don't think this pain will ever let up all I could do was scream to God was why me??? Then I heard a voice say why not you, I sacrificed my son to die for all of you, I created the heavens and the earth just like I created De'Mar. Every hair on his head, he was mines before he was yours. He is well, do not doubt my words. I have created a mansion here in heaven for everyone who believes in me and De'Mar believed in me, so he is well, his soul is well. I just sat there thinking my mind was playing tricks on me. I just wanted to wake up from this bad dream, but I was already awake, it wasn't a dream!

up. But that voice stuck in my head for some reason, it got me to at least focus, I still needed to be at that funeral.

God, I just ask for strength on the highway trying to get back there with my head hurting and hanging low. It is as if God was listening to my prayer. It was raining that day as we were traveling on the highway back to Rock Island for the funeral, the same highway that we've traveled countless number of times, under every type of weather condition. That day we seen something that we had never seen before. The rain had stopped, and suddenly, a rainbow appeared. You may be saying to yourself, we've all seen rainbows after a rain. Yes, that is true, but there was something different about this rainbow.

Usually, we see a rainbow in the distance, high in the sky. This rainbow appeared right beside us as if we could reach out and touch it. In all its vivid colors. While my husband is driving, and I am in the passenger seat, the rainbow is right outside my window, I can see it touching the road beside me. It was if God said to me in that moment, that you will be alright, your son is with me, his smile is with me. In that moment, I felt an overwhelming since of peace. I looked at my husband and we were both in awe of what God just showed us.

After that, I began to reflect back to what a Pastor had said to me, he told me don't forget I have other children and De'Mars children to share the memories with. Who was thinking about that? Not me. I just wanted my baby back. Although people may mean well, you would be surprised at some of the insensitive things that people say to you in moments like this, when you are grieving. Even if this is something they believe will help you like "God had a plan" really? I felt like slapping a woman for saying that to me. A plan for my child to die so young from a gunshot wound. Are you freaking kidding me? What God? Yeah, I was angry. Well, we stayed with my oldest son Darwin. It was very hard for me to do that. I couldn't get any sleep. Looking at him you could see the pain and hurt in his face every minute of the day.

constant worry and tears in fear of what we would do next. My oldest son did almost all the arrangements. He even helps with getting my son dressed. There's no way I could, my heart was broken. I just kept hoping it was a dream. It was hard enough for me to get through the day. So many people wanted to see me, to console me. I refused to see anyone. A couple of good friends ran into my sister, and she took them to my son's house knowing I didn't want to see anyone. I guess she thought they would help but nothing stops this pain!!! I met them outside, and of course they expressed their condolences. I couldn't say or do anything but cry. I would get so worked up, I started having panic attacks and I was ashamed to let people see me in this condition.

Ecclesiastes 3: There is a time for everything,
and a season for every activity under the heavens:
² *a time to be born and a time to die,*
a time to plant and a time to uproot,
³ *a time to kill and a time to heal,*
a time to tear down and a time to build,
⁴ *a time to weep and a time to laugh,*
a time to mourn and a time to dance,
⁵ *a time to scatter stones and a time to gather them,*
a time to embrace and a time to refrain from embracing,
⁶ *a time to search and a time to give up,*
a time to keep and a time to throw away,
⁷ *a time to tear and a time to mend,*
a time to be silent and a time to speak,
⁸ *a time to love and a time to hate,*
a time for war and a time for peace.

The morning of the funeral, what a day. It took me the longest to pull out that black dress. I bought this hat with a net on it to cover my face. I didn't even want to face people. I was sick to my stomach. I hadn't eaten anything for two days, so I was weak. I felt like I had lost weight. Why do people wear black to a funeral anyway? Is it out of respect or an old myth? But I guess times have changed because now I see this younger generation getting T-shirts made with the deceased person's face on it with a sense of love and respect, how times have changed. Someone called and asked my oldest son did we need a limo to pick the family up and bring them to the funeral. I said no I'll ride with my husband. We all proceeded to leave, headed to the church.

As we pulled up there were so many young adults outside the church, some screaming and crying, some across the street in groups smoking cigarettes and some with this angry and hurt look on their face. It took me 45 minutes to get out of the car. Jesse sat gather myself, but it turned into 45 minutes at least. We locked the car doors, so many walked up to the car to speak to me, but I had my head down blocking out everyone. His dad knocked on the window and asked me to roll down the window and said we have to see our son to say our last goodbye. I looked up at him and I saw nothing but De'Mar, they looked so much alike. My eyes welled up with tears, he reached his hand in the car and said let's walk together. Jesse helped me get out of the car and held me up as we walked to enter the church. A group of De'Mars friends walked up to me and said they were so sorry, he will truly be missed, I said thank you.

We finally made it up the steps inside the church someone had grabbed my other hand I looked down it was De'Mars oldest daughter, Damarius. I started crying and had another panic attack. They had to sit me down on a bench outside in the hall to calm me down. I finally calmed down enough, stood up again to make it in the church. When I started to walk down the aisle the casket was open. I see a glimpse of his face and started screaming to **God why**, You promised to keep my kids safe, I've done everything right, I've turned my life around, I believed in You, **why me** God. I just stood there for a minute screaming in pain, the Pastor had someone close the casket and have the mothers of the church help me down the aisle, they didn't think my husband and others were enough to get me to the front to my seat.

The church was so packed, it was people standing up in the choir stands and overflow of the church. There were at least six different Pastors that spoke along with many songs and so many young adults who wanted to speak on some memories. They also had this big screen that showed different clips of his pictures, it hurt to even lift my head up. All you heard were so many people behind me crying. I never turned around to look. We finally got to that last viewing. I couldn't look. Many people came by, then the last was family. I couldn't get up; it was like my legs and feet were numb. I just sat there in shock. Have you ever been in a dream and never get through this I just want to die right there with him. What do I have now? Ever since I've had children, my life and sacrifices I've made have been for them. The reverend touched me on the shoulder and said he had to close the casket. I said to close to it my baby is in heaven.

A flash back came over me for a second, the day he got baptized, which reflected on Gods promise. Once we turn our lives over and believe there is a God and get baptized, we are saved and were going to heaven. God built a place just for us once we leave this place. I felt someone tug on my arm. It was Jesse saying baby we need to go to the cemetery as the pallbearers were rolling out the casket. I rose to my feet and held on to him tight. As we walked out tears seemed like they were just planted on my face. I just couldn't stop, it's a pain that only someone with the same situation has endured. I think I'm going to just stay here. Why go home? This cemetery has my family here, my baby, my sister, nephew, and brothers.

Everything I've done, worked hard for trying to make a life for my children, it seems like I have failed them. I didn't care how I looked how much dirt was on me from sitting on the ground. Jesse said the day wasn't over and we still had to go to the repass. The father of one of De'Mar's friends owned a union hall, so he allowed us to have the repass there, out of the respect he had for De'Mar.

De'Mar's death affected so many young adults in and around the neighborhood and the Quad Cities. He touched so many lives, no matter where you live, or your status, he treated everyone with the utmost respect, and in turn, they loved and respected him for it. I walked into the hall, and it was a line out the door to get in. There was a table set up for immediate family in the front of the hall. I still couldn't believe this was happening but, I sat down, couldn't eat anything but many family members kept bringing me plates full of food and said that I needed to eat something. I can't. I'll take it back to the hotel. So many young men kept coming up near the memories they shared, at least not now!

I was going towards the bathroom and heard an argument towards the front entrance. I went to see where the commotion was coming from, looked out and it was my nephew arguing with De'Mars cousin on his dad's side. For those of you that have big families, you know there's at least one of them out of every group of 10 or so who get that liquid courage and want to fight everybody. Two things happen when you drink too much. You are either a happy drunk or an angry drunk. My nephew was an angry drunk who starts a mess all the time, which led me to believe that this happened because of him. My mother raised my two nephews, and she spoiled them rotten, they got away with everything and still do! They think things are supposed to be handed to them, they have not had a sustained legal job as of yet, at least at the time of this writing and we pray that changes for them.

I have also been told there was a confrontation at a club which involved one of them and the shooting started there and the enemies they had didn't care who they killed, as long as it was family. But so far, it's just a rumor. We haven't been able to prove it. People always tell rumors, but I have yet to see someone come forward to the police and tell them what happened.

The police tried to question my nephew. He keeps avoiding them I wonder why? I went out to the parking lot; it got quiet really quick. I walked towards my nephew and told him to leave, that he didn't deserve to be around the family and to add insult to injury it was my son's funeral. How dare you disrespect family, just leave don't be near here when I come back out. I couldn't do anything but walk away crying as others looked at me shaking their heads. It's hard enough to bury a child. I'm just trying get through the day, honestly the way I felt with a broken heart I could die in the next hour and wouldn't be surprised, as much pain as I felt since the day, I got that call. I was walking back into the building when my husband approached me saying he was just about to come find me, he was getting worried about me. We went served. I know it was at least 400 or more at the funeral and that's not including visitation, and at least 300 of them are De'Mar's age and friends he's either went to school with or came across meeting him. His smile and kindness, obviously he touched a lot of people. In my mind sitting there angry with God, after everything I gave Him, my whole life to protect my kids and He let me down. What do I do now? How do I live with this. Is it worth living for?

If I'm going to live, I got to stand up and do something. I refuse to let my son die in vain. This isn't normal, this is not going to be just another day. We had to stay and clean up after everything was over. I just appreciated De'Mars friend Dalton's father for letting us have the repass there for free. The only thing he asked for was to clean up afterwards. We were also truly grateful for how many people came together within such a small community to help pay for the arrangements. If you do not have life insurance, get some on you and all your children because you'll need it. Some Pastors of these churches don't sympathize with you, they just want to get paid even if you were a member of that church at a young age. They don't care, everything is based on money!!!! The Pastor of the church where we had the funeral even wanted money for the choir, and my husband had to leave the church to go get the money we left at our son's home.

He couldn't wait until the next day or even later that day. Sad, just sad. I just want to get back to the hotel and lie down. I know I can't go to sleep but at least I won't be around people looking in my face. Every time I lay down, I have nightmares, so sleep doesn't happen. After hugging so many people I'm truly worn out physically, mentally, and emotionally, nothing can comfort me. My heart is broken, it's like I'm here but in a bad nightmare I just can't wake up from.

*Psalms 37: [1] Do not fret because of those who are evil
or be envious of those who do wrong;
[2] for like the grass they will soon wither,
like green plants they will soon die away.*

I don't want to leave the rest of my children and grandchildren, but I can't stay in this city. It will haunt me for the rest of my life. I won't' stand by and let my child die in that way without doing anything. It hurts thinking of the pain he endured on the way to the hospital, so many emotions run through my body. It hurts so much; I look in the mirror and I don't understand why me God? What could I have done so bad to lose a son? How do I move forward? I know I'm going to need some help, mental help. How does a mother endure so much pain? I looked to the bible for answers, and God says what is meant for evil he'll turn it around for good. Am I reading that right? Well, why wasn't it stopped in the first place? God is supposed to be of love, so why isn't the ones that are trying to do right, the ones He save from evil? I'm just saying!!!! I'm confused.

On our way home I felt a sense of relief to not look behind me. It's another four-hour drive and all I want is some peace and quiet. If I go crazy with just the thoughts in my head, so be it! As long as it's not people in my ear telling me how sorry they are and if I ever need them just call. Well, that's a lie. I've seen people and family go on with their lives and don't even call to check on you!

Well, my journey is starting all over again. I thought everything was going well till this happened! After a silent ride we finally made it home and I couldn't be more relieved, not that I'm at peace, I just was very tired, and I didn't realize how much worry and lack of rest could take a toll on your body. But why can't I go to sleep and wake up in a dream where was just a nightmare, and everything is back to the way it was? Every time I get out of bed over again am I okay? Hell, no I'm not okay, my youngest son has died he can't call me no more, he can't say mom I love you anymore, I can't see that big smile that light up a bad day. I'm not alright! I know he means well, and I do not mean to take it out on him, and somehow, I know he understands, and he has been there for me through it all, and I love him for it. But what do I do with my anger, my broken heart and in so much pain that I have inside? How do I keep from blowing up and throwing things. I feel so helpless, I must stand up and fight back somehow.

Where do I start? I got all these people that came up to me saying they know what happened but won't go to the police! What's wrong with our people? Why are they so brain washed, even some of my own family members said they ain't no snitch they not going to the police. De'Mar always cherished family even the ones I couldn't trust! My nephew especially hung around him and De'Mar always had his back! My nephew caused more problems than a little bit, and De'Mar would be right there to save him. That same nephew who made the word disrespect a part of who he was.

As far as the situation with the loss of my son, I'm going to start by questioning and pressuring these police. I'm wondering how much do they really care? I'm never giving up until I get justice for my son, meaning the ones who did this are brought to justice. I am not looking for revenge, that's not what I want. I just want those responsible for my son's death to be legally held accountable. Someone knows something, but it's going take me going back home to get answers. I need to walk back through the neighborhood, to look around knocking on some doors. I drove back home to Shiloh, knowing I didn't want to ever go back to Rock Island again, but I refused to give up on finding out what happened to my son, and who was responsible. My mother told me to let go, and let God handle it. The way I was feeling, I trusted God with my children to keep them safe, and where did that get me. I didn't want to hear it. I know that as you read that, you might how can she say something like that? How can she say she is mad at God. I want to pause here and say, yes at that time, I was angry with God, distrustful of God. I was hurt, in shock, of losing my baby. All I will say here at this juncture of this book is, please be careful of judging. We all will have our crosses to bare, our storms to struggle with. You see, it's easy to say how we love and trust God, until He puts us to the test. The storm will do just that, put you through the test. How is your love for God, your faith in God when you are at your lowest, as I was.

I encourage you to read on, but I felt it important to share that here at this juncture in the book, because I know that I am not the only one to experience these feelings, and wanted people to know that because you have those feelings, does make you any less of a Christian. I wanted to be authentic with you, the reader.

Jeremiah 22: ³ This is what the LORD says: Do what is just and right. Rescue from the hand of the oppressor the one who has been robbed. Do no wrong or violence to the foreigner, the fatherless or the widow, and do not shed innocent blood in this place.

Back home for answers. As me, my husband and my oldest son Darwin walked through the neighborhood questioning the ones who would be brave enough to open the door, I explained who I was, some of them didn't mind talking. As we noticed it starting to get dark, I asked one of the elderly ladies that had been living close to the alley where my son died, why is it so dark on the front streets? She said none of the streetlights worked and they hadn't been working for a couple of years. Every time she complained to the alderman, he did not do anything about it, and she felt that they were being ignored.

Well, that started a fire in me, I was upset hearing that! I told my son Darwin maybe if there had been some lights and cameras the perpetrators who committed the crimes would be caught, or not so quick to do it in a lighted area. So, the next day I went down to city hall and asked who would I speak to about the streetlights? They gave me the run around. You understand what I mean, they started sending me to this person, and that person sends you to the next person, not assisting me with finding the right person to address the issue/concern. Finally, I asked to speak to the City Manager. I spoke with him regarding that neighborhood and how I was concerned about the streetlights not working.

He began by saying I should get the alderman involved, he was fully in charge of that neighborhood. I proceeded to tell him the neighborhood already tried that. I started telling him, the City Manager who I was and what this meant to me and the look on my face showed I wasn't going to accept no as an answer, and I was going to be around until I got some answers. He asked me if the mayor about our conversation, and he informed me that the mayor's response was, the last set of lights that were there were shot out by drug dealers and the best thing to do was put a petition together for the neighborhood to sign on. If I got enough signatures, they would present it at the city monthly meeting to vote on it. This meeting is also open to the public to attend.

So, I solicited help from some friends, children, family and my husband, and we went knocking on doors all through that neighborhood and got the required number of signatures and beyond. I ended up with over 800 signatures. People wanted change but didn't know where to start and they had already given up on the Alderman that was assigned for that neighborhood. They had just lost all faith and confidence in him. I went to the next public meeting. I wanted to see what it was all about and see how they were going to vote on the lights, pushing my pain and suffering aside, I was there front and center, with some family members, mainly my son, one sister, and my husband.

Genesis 37: [34] Then Jacob tore his clothes, put on sackcloth and mourned for his son many days. [35] All his sons and daughters came to comfort him, but he refused to be comforted. "No," he said, "I will continue to mourn until I join my son in the grave." So his father wept for him.

My mind has been going back and forth, from the night of the tragedy to present day, some days are better than others. There are times though, that I started blaming myself, my mind would wonder in some of the most dangerous places, even thinking about killing the people who done this. I thought about hurting myself, being gone from this horrible world. People live off jealousy, hate, discrimination, and the power to take over something that's not theirs. I just wanted to give up. I don't know if it was because I was extra sensitive because of the murder of my son or not, but it seemed that right after De'Mar was murdered there were a rash of shootings in the Quad Cities. I'm numb every morning God wakes me up. I keep asking him in a stern voice why am I in this position? I hear Pastor, Reverends say (what was meant for evil God will turn for good, for those who love him) Romans 8:28. I'm still looking for the good, my baby's gone. In my mind, the way I was feeling at the time was the only good would be is God bringing him back like Lazarus.

This city meeting went on and on but once, I finally spoke on behalf of that neighborhood, there wasn't no question of what was needed so they agreed. It felt good to accomplish something productive for that neighborhood but that wasn't bringing my baby back. The labor pain's carrying him and nurturing him to the man he had become and not deserving the pain he must have felt. I think about what some people told me, rumors I believe. Some of the rumors came from my daughters' children's father. During that time, I did not trust him.

loss of other siblings, a divorce to a man I thought I would be with for the rest of my life, losing my grandma who suffered from dementia, all that pain will never amount to losing a child. This is a pain you don't wish on no one. What mind set does a person have to have to literally take someone's life and just keep living with no remorse? I'm thinking a mind that's mentally challenged to think you are not going to reap what you sow. I remember back in the day when I was raised, if me and another person had a disagreement and wanted to fight, we fought and were friends the next day. I'm not saying that's what it was but, man I wish this young generation today would think twice before they react, before they pull out a gun and take a life. It's as if they do not think about how their actions affect not just the person they are killing, but how it affects that person's family. Black people fought so hard for each other as slaves to be free and take care of one another. Now we're killing each other senselessly.

My mind keeps going back to De'Mars children that are left behind without a father. What world do we live in when we must tell our children their parents are gone and never coming back. Have we ever sat back and thought how it affects children, the questions they ask and how it's very hard for them to understand at that age. Missing so many special moments like, daughter daddy dances, no daddy to speak to when you need advice, no daddy to protect you. I could go on and on, but it will not get rid of the pain they have to face. The pain will last a lifetime and they will be sharing that pain every time someone asks them where's your dad because it will always come up. Parents are a valuable part of your life. Once you lose them a piece of you is lost forever. Every time I look at De'Mars kids, I see him.

I'm not going out like this, I must stand up and fight for him, for his justice, for his legacy. I'm starting to realize why black woman are always at the fore front fighting. This goes all the way back to slavery fighting for freedom, and justice. I keep asking God every time I cry, why me? I'm waiting for an answer. I'm so keep coming up to me with pity on their face and those same words I'm sorry for your loss, offering their condolences. And the younger generation who hung around him who knew him cry every time they see me. I taught my children to always respect your elders and help people, that's where your blessings come from. So De'Mar was known for doing just that.

I didn't realize I hadn't eaten anything; my appetite is just gone! I'm on my way to the police station to stay on them and help them build a case because the neighborhood is saying they don't care about solving any crimes in the neighborhood, especially if you're a black family. Well, they're going to get sick of me because I'm going to be there until something is done. Amid all this I didn't realize my blood pressure was up, stress level was through the roof, and there was no sleep. Jesse called our primary doctor and explained what happened. He prescribed me some sleeping and anxiety pills. The thought in my head is saying just take all of them and be done, but I keep looking at the rest of my children trying to be strong in front of them, but at night I let it all out. My oldest son hears screaming and crying, as Jesse tries to console me. Every time I try to dose off to sleep, I see my baby laying there, so I scream for help and that wakes me up.

I never thought I would have such horrible nightmares, but these nightmares are so real. I'll sit up and cry instead of lying down until I see daylight. I want to go back to where he fell and just sit there and cry, but my body won't let me go back to that place. I hate being in this town, but I have unfinished business to do here. There's a church right in the neighborhood. They have a woman Pastor, the same one who spoke so eloquently and spoke of helping the neighborhood during the vigil. I'm going to ask If there were any cameras at their church that may have caught something that might help?

Matthew 25: [34] *"Then the King will say to those on his right, 'Come, you who are blessed by my Father; take your inheritance, the kingdom prepared for you since the creation of the world.* [35] *For I was hungry and you gave me something to eat, I was thirsty and you gave me something to drink, I was a stranger and you invited me in,* [36] *I needed clothes and you clothed me, I was sick and you looked after me, I was in prison and you came to visit me.'*

[37] *"Then the righteous will answer him, 'Lord, when did we see you hungry and feed you, or thirsty and give you something to drink?* [38] *When did we see you a stranger and invite you in, or needing clothes and clothe you?* [39] *When did we see you sick or in prison and go to visit you?'*

[40] *"The King will reply, 'Truly I tell you, whatever you did for one of the least of these brothers and sisters of mine, you did for me.'*

Months have passed, life goes on, I'm back home in Shiloh, everyone is back to work, dealing with their own lives. The silence is deafening, no one is around, it is just me and my thoughts, and that is sometimes unbearable. Not noticing that my health was failing every day. God woke me up. I used to say, thank God for waking me up. But for what? At this point in my life, I felt it was over, anyhow. I didn't care whether I woke up or not. I heard a pastor say to me, you still have so much and so many to live for. My response was they would be alright, until one morning, I woke up in a cold sweat and head throbbing. I tried to open my eyes, and my eyesight was blurry, and I couldn't see at all out of my left eye. I thought maybe it was matted shut from the tears. I shouted Jesse's name and told him what I was going through, and he assured me my eyes were open.

I told him that my eyesight was blurry in my right eye, and I couldn't see at all out of my left eye. He calmed me down to a the emergency room. It was there that I found out that I was on the verge of a stroke. The doctor informed me that my blood pressure was sky high, and my blood glucose was high as well, all of which was impacting my eyesight. I was given instructions to rest, and try to reduce the amount of stress, and some pain medicine for my headache. When I got home, all I could do was get upstairs and try to sleep off the trauma. I didn't care once again about waking up. I was almost there anyhow, with those results from the doctor. Finally, and for the first time since I lost my son, I fell into a deep sleep. I dreamed I was in the movie theater, and as I got up to leave the theater, I started walking up the aisle with my head down to watch my step.

It was still slightly dark, and as I lifted my head, there was De'Mar standing there, tall as ever, looking in my eyes, but looking younger by maybe a few years. He leaned his forehead down to touch mine. He said in a calm voice. Mom, I'm alright. I'm OK. It's going to be OK. I said, I love you. He hugged me and turned around and started to walk away. I tried reaching out to grab him, but the further away he got, the more he faded out of my sight. I woke up with tears on my face. God said in a small voice. You will have peace.

What do I do? I need help. I need some guidance, but not just any guidance. I will seek spiritual guidance. That is just what I did. I prayed about it, and God led me to my Ministering Evangelist. We would meet twice a week for approximately three months. Then I sought out Baptist pastors for the next year. All of this spiritual guidance really helped me. Honestly, I wouldn't have made it if it wasn't for Godley council. As a result of this spiritual guidance, I was able to let go of my anger at God, read the Bible for answers, and share my struggles with other mothers who lost a child. I was able to seek out groups and share my testimony to whomever wanted to listen. I still struggle but I get up every morning and ask God for strength and peace to make it another day. I also developed a better understanding of God's promises.

unexpected ways. Not long after we lost our son in August, around October of that same year (just a few months later) one of my husband's softball teammates experienced the exact same thing. Their son was shot and killed. Even though we were still grieving our loss, we were able to be there for our friends. I am not saying that we were able to stop their pain, because there is no stopping that, we were able to give them a shoulder to cry on, we were able to honestly say, *"I understand your pain"* having just endured our loss. We were able to have conversations with them, we were able to sympathize with them, share with them how we got through, share with them our struggles, and yes share with them how we questioned God.

People sometimes frown when they hear that people question God. There's a difference when you say questioned God and stopped believing in God. We didn't stop believing in God, we just had questions. I don't expect everyone to understand, and I pray if you are reading this, that you will never have to endure the pain of losing a child. It's just that kind of pain caused me to question God. Even though I did, I never lost faith, I never lost my praise. I know that it was God who got me through this, or else I would not have made it. And that is what my husband and I were able to share with this couple. My husband supported him, and I supported the wife. God said, I brought you through, I am holding you up, now go share that with others, and that is what we did. To this day, we remain close and check on one another, especially on holidays, birthdays, etc. Holidays are some of the roughest times, especially the initial holiday after your loss.

If that wasn't enough, about two years after I lost my son, I got a call from my sister telling me that my nephew (her son) committed suicide. You can only imagine the rush of emotion that came over me. He had shot himself in the head in front of her home. She was devastated to say the least. This brought back a flood of memories. You see, this is not the first time that my family has endured suicide. After the loss of my eldest sister, her brothers two boys. As a result, the youngest of my sister's sons never felt the love he longed for from his mother and it impacted him deeply, and he committed suicide at the age of 12. His brothers left my mother's home to live with other family members and have returned to visit but not stay, and that was over 25 years ago.

Now fast forward to the present, my sister called on me to take care of everything, saying she just could not do it. I had to put my grieving aside, not just for my son, but for my nephew now to help my sister through this tragedy. So back to Rock Island, where I truly hate to be other than to visit my mother, other children, and grandchildren. I was hesitant to go, remembering how no one was there for me, especially my sisters. I put all of that aside to go put things in place to help my grieving sister. How did I do it you ask, nobody but God. God gave me the strength to do what had to be done, and we were able to get through it.

God wasn't finish with me then and He is not finished with me now. He continues to be my strength, so much so, that I got up and started moving, started doing things. I became a spokeswoman for mothers losing a child. I spoke at different events, even traveling to Chicago speaking, sharing my story, and working with moms that are fighting for justice and speaking out against gun violence. I started building a legacy for my son, for his three beautiful daughters who must grow up without their dad. Although they may have to grow up without him, they will grow up knowing about him.

We continued to meet with the Rock Island police department to stay on them, about the case, however, we have gotten nowhere. It is as if they lost interest over the years, however, we remain faithful, and know that God is still in charge and in His time, we will receive justice for our son. We tried all we could with appeals and letters etc., moving ahead of God, but he told us to be still and know that He is God, and He is in control. So, my focus shifted to our son's legacy. It has been seven years on getting justice, we just know that it will come.

Some things that we have accomplished in my son's name are:

- 2016 we hosted a candlelight prayer vigil here is a link you can use to view it.

  https://wqad.com/2016/08/29/vigil-calls-for-a-stop-to-gun-violence-after-rock-island-man-shot-to-death/

- 2016 we hosted a free community breakfast and invited (city officials) to address community concerns.

- 2016 – present, continue to hold a multitude of speaking engagement's

- 2016 – present, we established our own Prayer Line (319) 527-9690 that is open to the country on Mon/Wed nights that start at 8:15 PM central standard time. This was established to help the young adults who were struggling with the grief they were feeling after the loss of De'Mar.

- 2017 hosted a fundraiser to pay for the memorial bench.

- 2017 honored De'Mar with an honorary memorial bench on the side of Church of Peace, in Rock Island, IL.

- 2017- present, continue to to maintain awareness by putting up billboards throughout the year (maintaining awareness of gun violence).

- 2018 hosted a De'Mar De'Angelo Bester Unity Day Resource Event to bring awareness of all available resources for the community.

- 2018 worked with UnityPoint Health Trinity Hospital in Rock Island, IL, to have a window built for viewing deceased loved ones, and developed a Compassion

- 2019 hosted a Men's Walk of Faith

- 2019 worked with UnityPoint Health Trinity Hospital to develop a video to help educate staff on how families are impacted during a sudden tragedy, to improve how such events can be handled with compassion. They now have a video with me and my eldest son sharing our story of the night he died. It is required viewing for new hires to understand how their actions affect loved ones of the people they care for in that type of situation.

- 2019 proposed to the City Council an "Adopt a Block" program.

- 2020, worked with City of Rock Island to have an Honorary Street name change to (De'Mar's Way) and on May 5th, 2020, this became a reality

- Future endeavors include establishing a resource center in De'Mars name to be located in Rock Island, IL.

- 2020-present looking to purchase a building in Rock Island, IL to help families get the appropriate resources. Eventually establish a grief center.

- 2022 – Present, along with husband, host Grief Share both in person at our church and online.

- 2024 – anticipate completion and publishing of book outlining my story

Email: otheastevenson17@gmail.com

Prayer Line email: stevensonsprayerline@gmailcom

Prayer line call in number (319) 527-9690…the prayer line is active Mondays, and Wednesdays beginning at 8:15 pm central standard time.

Lifelong Experiences website (scan the QR code)

Instagram: Othea Stevenson

Linked In: Othea Stevenson

Facebook: Othea Stevenson

As you can see, God has given me the strength to move forward. I'm often asked, how do you do it, how can you do all that you are doing after your loss. I am quick to share with them, I can't. It is God working in and through me that allows me to do so. If it were not for God, I truly believe, I would not have made it this far. I continue to lean on God each day. Each day God blesses me to wake up, and then I ask for peace.

Do I struggle at times? Absolutely, but God calms my spirit, and I am able to move on. I will share with anyone, the pain never goes away, God gives us the strength to deal with it each day. There are days that I am strong, and there are days that I am weak, but each and every day, God is stronger still, and that is what I hold to, and that is what I share on my prayer line, that is what I share with anyone who will listen, and that is what I share with you who are reading this book.

I encourage anyone who is going through or has gone through something similar, you first have my heartfelt condolences. I would encourage you to lean on God, and to share your testimony. I found that sharing my story has been therapeutic, but most of all I'm trusting in God's word (the Bible) to share how He has brought me through. I wish you all love, peace, and the comfort of God. May God Bless you all.

Agape Love,
Othea Stevenson

Initial billboard

Othea Stevenson is a business owner, teacher, community activist, motivational speaker, and a mother of four. She was raised in the Quad Cities, and she is now on a mission from God to work towards the betterment of the community by working to dispel the negative perceptions of the community, fighting for the rights of the community, and seeking justice for her son.

made it her life's work to better a neighborhood, improve a city and work with a hospital to better deal with grieving families."

John Marx of
The Dispatch and The Rock Island Argus
Monday, April 20, 2020